To

faithfully

Elton Trueblow

THE HUMOR OF CHRIST

nov. 17, 1983

THE
HUMOR
OF
CHRIST

Elton Trueblood

Published in San Francisco by
HARPER & ROW, PUBLISHERS
New York, Hagerstown, San Francisco, London

LIBRARY OF CONGRESS CATALOG CARD NUMBER: 75-12280

ISBN: 0-06-068632-4

85 86   10 9 8 7

To Martin, who knew when to laugh

Contents

Preface

The germ of the idea which has finally led to the writing of this book was planted many years ago when our eldest son was four years old. We were reading to him from the seventh chapter of Matthew's Gospel, feeling very serious, when suddenly the little boy began to laugh. He laughed because he saw how preposterous it would be for a man to be so deeply concerned about a speck in another person's eye, that he was unconscious of the fact his own eye had a beam in it. Because the child understood perfectly that the human eye is not large enough to have a beam in it, the very idea struck him as ludicrous. His gay laughter was a rebuke to his parents for their failure to respond to humor in an unexpected place. The rebuke served its purpose by causing me to begin to watch for humor in all aspects of the life and teachings of Christ. Sometimes this did not appear until the text had been read and reread many times.

Finally, after many years, it became clear to me that I ought to try to write something that would help to overcome an almost universal failure to appreciate an element in Christ's life which is so important that, without it, any understanding of Him is inevitably distorted. At first I thought that this might be done in a single chapter, but, as I studied the subject more thoroughly, I came to realize that an entire book would be required. This is because the general misunderstanding is very great, and also because much of the relevant evidence is so deeply hidden by accepted presuppositions that it will not be recognized apart from some analysis. The plan, as it developed, was as follows: It is necessary, first, to do something to challenge the conventionalized picture of a Christ who never laughed, and this can be done by reference to deeds as well as to words. Next it is helpful to try to analyze the character of Christ's humor, with reference to humor in general. This prepares us for a consideration of the type of humor found most widely in the Gospels, that of irony. The book ends with an analysis of three particular ways in which Christ's humor is employed, first, in controversy, second, in parables, and third, in a short dialogue. The list of passages printed in the Appendix is provided in order to assist the studious reader who wishes to refer directly to passages mentioned in the text.

We do not know with certainty how much humor there is in Christ's teaching, but we can be sure that there is far more than is normally recognized. In any case there are numerous passages in the recorded teaching which are practically incomprehensible when regarded as sober prose, but which are luminous once we become liberated from the gratuitous assumption that Christ never joked. In some cases the recognition of humor is a genuine solvent. We have heard much, and possibly too much, in our generation, of demythologizing the Gospels; perhaps there is a parallel process which is more fruitful, though we have no catchword for it. This is the process of freeing the Gospel from the excessive sobriety which is provided both by the authors and by us. Once we realize that Christ was not always engaged in pious talk, we have made an enormous step on the road to understanding.

It is generally recognized today that the quest for the historical Jesus is, in some sense, a frustrating one. Schweitzer has convinced us that a simple return to the authentic historical record is impossible. While, on the one hand, there is no case at all for the denial of historicity, there is, on the other hand, no possibility of a definitive life of Jesus. While we are grateful for the partial history which we have, modern scholarship has made us see that the purpose of our Gospels is evangelical rather than historical. This is what is meant by emphasis on the Kerygmatic. It is almost a truism to say that men preached *about* Christ before they knew, in any detail, either what He said or what He did. It is probable that we know more of the details of the life of Jesus than was known even by the Apostle Paul. If there is any conclusion on which contemporary New Testament scholars are agreed, it is that men preached about the resurrected Christ before there was the demand for knowledge of Christ's earthly life which led to the production of the Gospels as we know them. We have an advantage which Paul at Corinth did not have—we can read the Gospels!

By a kind of inevitability we have moved, in contemporary scholarship, away from the destructive antithesis, which seemed to suggest that almost everything in the Gospels was myth, without returning to uncritical acceptance of every account. This new synthesis is represented brilliantly in the work of Professor Gunther Bornkamm, of the University of Heidelberg, particularly in his work *Jesus of Nazareth*. "Quite clearly," he concludes, "what the Gospels report concerning the message, the deeds and the history of Jesus is still distinguished by an authenticity, a freshness, and a distinctiveness not in any way effaced by the Church's Easter faith." We do not know all that Jesus said or did, but we know something. This is enough to make the search for His humor a valid enterprise.

The literate reader will notice that I make, in this book, no serious effort to distinguish between the *ipsissima verba* of Jesus and the possible or probable additions or phrasing provided by the authors of the Gospels. This is not to say that I do not respect the achievements of those who are engaged in this effort, including those who are working studiously to provide effective form criticism. It *is* to say that such an effort, in any detail, is beyond the scope and purpose of this book, as it is also beyond the competence of the author.

The reader will, I hope, understand why I have entitled the book *The Humor of Christ,* instead of calling it The Humor of Jesus. This is partly because I do not think any sharp or absolute distinction can be made, or needs to be made, between the Jesus of History and the Christ of Faith. I have employed the word "Christ" because that is what most people in the modern world call Him. I agree with the linguistic philosophers in their desire to use the language of ordinary people whenever and wherever such language is not confusing. Also I happen to believe that He was and is the One who truly reveals the Father to us. I understand why some authors do not capitalize pronouns referring to Him, but I feel more loyal when I employ such capitalization.

The quotations from the Bible which appear in this volume are from the Revised Standard Version, unless otherwise noted. Because the book touches, in a modest way, upon New Testament scholarship, I have been very glad that my friend and colleague, Dr. Alexander C. Purdy, long occupant of the Hosmer Chair of New Testament at Hartford Theological Seminary, has given the text the benefit of his critical reading. Though this was a necessary safeguard, in view of the fact that the New Testament has not been my chief field of study, it will be obvious to the reader that this book is written more in the mood of a philosopher than in that of a New Testament critic. Philosophy has long been concerned with laughter, and a significant part of the field is the one studied here.

E. T.

Pen Point
Greentown, Pennsylvania

THE HUMOR OF CHRIST

CHAPTER I

❧ ❦

A Neglected Aspect

Do not look dismal.
Matthew 6:16

THE WIDESPREAD FAILURE to recognize and to appreciate the humor of Christ is one of the most amazing aspects of the era named for Him. Anyone who reads the Synoptic Gospels with a relative freedom from presuppositions might be expected to see that Christ laughed, and that He expected others to laugh, but our capacity to miss this aspect of His life is phenomenal. We are so sure that He was always deadly serious that we often twist His words in order to try to make them conform to our preconceived mold. A misguided piety has made us fear that acceptance of His obvious wit and humor would somehow be mildly blasphemous or sacrilegious. Religion, we think, is serious business, and serious business is incompatible with banter.

The critics of Christ have, on the whole, been as blind to His humor as have His admirers. Even Nietzsche, in deploring Christ's early death, wrote, "Would that he had remained in the wilderness and far from the good and just! Perhaps he would have learned to live and to love the earth—and laughter too."[1] The supposedly fierce critic was thus uncritical in that

[1] Translation of Nietzsche's "Live Dangerously" by Walter Kaufmann, in the latter's *Existentialism from Dostoevsky to Sartre* (New York: Meridian Books, 1956), p. 109.

he did not bother to go beyond the stereotype to examine the evidence objectively.

The fact is that we have often developed a false pattern of Christ's character. Though we do not always say so directly, we habitually think of Him as mild in manner, endlessly patient, grave in speech, and serious almost to the point of dourness. The evidence for this is that we try to explain away any words or incidents in the Gospels which are inconsistent with such a picture. But, if we abandon this effort, and "sit down before the fact as a little child," with a minimum of presupposition, we come out with a radically different conception.

The supposed mildness is contradicted in a spectacular manner by the attack on the Pharisees. If the twenty-third chapter of Matthew were required reading, part of the stereotype would be broken, for few of us have heard in our day any attack so scathing, even in the midst of a political campaign. Christ apparently adopted from John the Baptist the choice epithet "brood of vipers" (Matt. 3:7 and Matt. 23:33), but He went on to manufacture stronger epithets of His own. Can a man be called a worse name than a white-washed tomb, full of putrid and decaying flesh? There is nothing mild about saying, as Matthew reports in two different contexts (Matt. 5:29, 30 and 18:8, 9), that there are situations in which a man ought to pluck out his eye and cut off his hand and throw them away. Nor is there mildness in Mark 9:43-48, which concludes with the violent double metaphor, "where their worm does not die, and the fire is not quenched."

The fiction that Christ was endlessly patient will not bear examination. In His impatience with His inept disciples He is reported as saying, "How much longer must I endure you?" (Matt. 17:17, N.E.B.). In the parable of the Barren Fig Tree (Luke 13:6-9) we have a vivid account of the divine impatience. The clear teaching is that it is reasonable to be patient

for a while, in order to give the unfruitful person or unpro-
ductive organization a chance, but that there is a limit to the
required patience, and that, when we go beyond this limit,
tolerance ceases to be a virtue. It is all right, we are told, to put
on manure for one more year, but no longer.[2]

Christ's teaching to the effect that externals, including foods,
cannot possibly make an inner or spiritual difference is stated
with vivid emphasis as follows: "Listen to me, all of you, and
understand this: nothing that goes into a man from outside
can defile him; no, it is the things that come out of him that
defile a man" (Mark 7:14, 15, N.E.B.). Since the boldness of
this approach confused the literal-minded disciples, they asked
for clarification and, this time, Christ was even more direct,
speaking openly of the fact of evacuation. "He said to them,
'Are you as dull as the rest? Do you not see that nothing that
goes from outside into a man can defile him, because it does
not enter into his heart but into his stomach, and so passes
out into the drain?'" (Mark 7:18, 19, N.E.B.). All evils, He
thus taught, have internal origins. The deepest sins are spiritual rather than physical.

A prosy literalism not only misses the wry humor, when
humor is present, but, what is worse, misses the point of the
teaching. Christ taught in figures nearly all of the time, and
everyone knows that no figure is to be accepted in its entirety.
No one could suppose that when Jesus said He was the door,
He meant that He was made of wood. Most figures exist in
order to illustrate single points, and to illustrate them with the
requisite vividness. Thus each becomes patently absurd when
it is pressed too far. The very fact that such figures are necessarily limited gives each one of them a little touch of humor.
For example, there is sly humor, as well as deep meaning, in

[2] The parable of the Barren Fig Tree is unique to Luke and is in no way
identical with the cursing of the fig tree (Matt. 21:18, 19 and Mark 11:12-14)
which is reported as an event. The narrative may be a confusion of the parable.

Christ's words about where to put a light. The message is about the necessity of witness, but the failure to make a witness is rendered laughable when Jesus asks, "Is a lamp brought in to be put under a bushel, or under a bed, and not on a stand?" (Mark 4:21). Since the lamp mentioned has an open flame and since the bed is a mattress, it is easy to see that in this situation the light would be suffocated or the mattress would be burned. The appeal here is to the patently absurd. The sensitive laugh, because they get the point.

The sly insertions are numerous indeed. In the midst of a serious discourse, the theme is lightened by the observation, "But know this, that if the householder had known at what hour the thief was coming, he would have been awake and would not have left his house to be broken into" (Luke 12:39). All of us know that it is easy to be smart when we are tipped off, and that to be forewarned is to be forearmed, but Christ delights us, in this case, by a fresh statement of the obvious. All of us know that we are sometimes more concerned with the social effects of our actions, in terms of reputation, than we are with intrinsic right and wrong, but we recognize this more vividly when Christ points out the tendency to cleanse the outside of the cup, rather than the inside (Matt. 23:25-26).

One reason for our failure to laugh is our extreme familiarity with the received text. The words seem to us like old coins, in which the edges have been worn smooth and the engravings have become almost indistinguishable. This is particularly true of the words of the Authorized Version. The words seem so hallowed that they deepen the force of inherited assumptions, which may actually be contrary to fact. In this situation the newer translations are often helpful. These are more likely to make us see the paradoxical character of what has come to be accepted as common and unexciting. But we need more than new translations; we need a definite act of will. The main effort must be an effort on the part of the contemporary student to confront Christ as actually portrayed rather than as we have imagined Him to be. Only then will we feel the sharpness of His wit. We must do something to liberate our minds from "the spell of familiar and venerated words" in order to see their true significance. When we do so it is impossible to argue with Edith Hamilton in her trenchant dictum about the Gospels. "When they are read with serious attention," she writes, "the kind of study one gives to something to be mastered, the result is startling."[3]

A second reason for our widespread failure to recognize the humor of the Gospels is their great stress upon the tragedy of the crucifixion and the events immediately preceding it. The events of the final days are told with such fullness that a stranger to our culture, coming to the Gospels without preparation, might be excused for thinking of them as the story of Christ's passion, with introductory passages added. The events of Good Friday and Easter, because of their dramatic appeal and profound significance, began, very early in Christian history, to occupy the center of interest. Because the tragic aspect is intrinsically unhumorous, men came to see the sad picture as the whole picture. When artists began to produce speculative portraits of Christ they naturally stressed the somber aspect. How many of the well-known efforts to portray Christ show Him laughing or presenting a witty paradox? By enormous good luck the authors of the Synoptic Gospels were able to preserve the authentic account which His simple followers had provided, but, as the Fourth Gospel shows, the further men got from such sources, the less humor there was. The contrast between John and the Synoptics is, in this regard, striking indeed. The Apostle Paul, who never knew Christ in the flesh, appears to reflect none of Christ's humor. Indeed, the contrast in humor is one of the deepest contrasts between the Synoptic

[3] Edith Hamilton, *Witness to the Truth* (New York: W. W. Norton & Company, 1948), p. 13.

Gospels and the writings of Paul. Though Paul could be eloquent, he appears to have lacked Christ's gift of witty speech.

We have many reasons for being grateful for the production of the Synoptic Gospels, but one of the greatest reasons is that they provide a powerful antidote to the subsequent distortion. The Person they present has many contrasting features. He is a Man of Sorrows, but He is also a Man of Joys; He uses terribly rough and blunt language; He expresses blazing anger; He teases; He foregathers with a gay crowd. How, for example, could we ever miss the fact that His words and behavior surprised His contemporaries? We are told that "they were surprised that words of such grace should fall from his lips" (Luke 4:22, N.E.B.)

That Christ went with the gay crowd, including what the New English Bible calls "many bad characters," was extremely shocking to the religious leaders. Could there be any depth to His teaching if He failed to see how unworthy these laughing people were! "Now the tax collectors and sinners were all drawing near to him. And the Pharisees and the scribes murmured, saying, 'This man receives sinners and eats with them'" (Luke 15:1, 2). While Luke alone gives us the choice bit just quoted, all the Synoptics give the story of the feast at Levi's house. Mark's rendering is:

And as he sat at table in his house, many tax collectors and sinners were sitting with Jesus and his disciples; for there were many who followed him. And the scribes of the Pharisees when they saw that he was eating with sinners and tax collectors, said to his disciples, "Why does he eat with tax collectors and sinners?" And when Jesus heard it, he said to them, "Those who are well have no need of a physician, but those who are sick; I came not to call the righteous, but sinners." [Mark 2:15-17]

That Christ did not fit the expected pattern was clear. Those who gathered around John the Baptist, like those who followed the Pharisaic party, engaged in solemn fasts, but Christ did not do so. Both He and His disciples were notable for their eating and drinking (Luke 5:33). Though only his enemies called Him a drunkard, it is obvious that Christ drank wine. It was His general reputation for gaiety which provided the basis for one of His most humorous rejoinders, to the effect that the critics could not be pleased. If people did not like the abstemiousness of John, and if they also did not like the gaiety of Jesus, what *did* they want?

"To what then shall I compare the men of this generation, and what are they like? They are like children sitting in the market place and calling to one another,

'We piped to you, and you did not dance;
we wailed, and you did not weep.'

For John the Baptist has come eating no bread and drinking no wine; and you say, 'He has a demon.' The Son of Man has come eating and drinking; and you say, 'Behold, a glutton and a drunkard, a friend of tax collectors and sinners!' Yet wisdom is justified by all her children." [Luke 7:31-35]

The sharp thrust of this final line is characteristic of Christ's sly humor. He is willing to rest the case in terms of human consequences. What happens in the lives of men and women is the real test of His position or any other. His bad reputation among the pious is a trivial matter, provided the lives of ordinary people are enriched and glorified. "I'll judge by my consequences, if you will judge by yours," He is saying in the most pithy manner.

Perhaps our greatest failure in creating a false picture of Christ has been a failure of logic. We assume that an assertion of sadness entails a denial of humor, but there is no good reason to suppose that such is the case. There is abundant evidence to show that contrasting elements of character, far from being mutually incompatible, are often complementary. The fact that Christ laughed does not, and need not, mean that He did not also weep. It is a well-known fact that humor often appears in the most noble spirits. Indeed, it is hard to find genuine classics without this combination. An excellent contemporary illustration of the fertile combination of seriousness and humor is provided by that inimitable journal, *The New Yorker*. Real humor, instead of being something merely light or superficial, depends upon profundity. "A humorous rejoinder," said Kierkegaard, "must always contain something profound."[4] Greatness is denied to those termed by Kierkegaard the "stupidly serious."

That mirth and compassion are compatible is one of the greatest lessons mankind can learn. Lincoln, before he read to the cabinet his draft of the Emancipation Proclamation, eased tensions by reading from a humorous book. The fact that he was a notable teller of funny stories did not hinder, in the least, his expression of profound pathos in the Second Inaugural. We can say of him, as Macaulay said of Addison, that he possessed "a mirth consistent with tender compassion for all that is frail, and with profound reverence for all that is sublime."

Boswell's *Life of Johnson* is generally regarded as the greatest of all biographical works, and part of the reason for this reputation is its remarkable ability to shift from the sublime to the laughable. One of the reasons why all Western philosophy is a continuation of the heritage of Socrates is that the great Athenian exhibited precisely the combination in which humor and seriousness strengthen each other. Who, having once read the *Apology*, for example, can forget the way in which Socrates, facing his accusers and recognizing that he was doomed, made a laughable and preposterous proposal about his penalty. The penalty he suggested was entertainment for life at the Prytaneum, a dining hall in Athens maintained at public expense.[5]

[4] Søren Kierkegaard, *Concluding Unscientific Postscript*, tr. by David F. Swenson (Princeton: Princeton University Press, 1941), p. 491 n.
[5] *Apology*, 36E.

It was at the Prytaneum that distinguished citizens were enter-
tained. He even joked in the hour of his death, when Crito
asked how they should bury him. " 'Any way you like,' replied
Socrates, 'that is, if you can catch me and I don't slip through
your fingers.' He laughed gently as he spoke, and turning to us
went on, 'I can't persuade Crito that I am this Socrates here
who is talking to you now and marshalling all the arguments.
He thinks I am the one whom he will see presently lying dead,
and he asks how he is to bury me!' "[6]
Far from laughter being incompatible with anguish, it is
often the natural expression of deep pain. Coleridge faced this
clearly when he tried to see why Hamlet jests when his companions overtake him. "Terror," he says, "is closely connected
with the ludicrous; the latter is the common mode by which
the mind tries to emancipate itself from terror. The laugh is
rendered by nature itself the language of extremes, even as
tears are."[7] It is not possible to have genuine humor or true wit
without an extremely sound mind, which is always a mind
capable of high seriousness and a sense of the tragic. This is
obviously part of the meaning of Socrates when, after a full
night of discussion with Agathon and his other friends, including even Alcibiades, he ended the symposium, at daybreak,
by insisting that anyone who can write tragedy can also write
comedy, because the fundamental craft is the same in each of
them. Kierkegaard echoed this conclusion when he said that
the comic and the tragic touch each other at the absolute point
of infinity.

An appealing example which shows that wit and seriousness
are wholly compatible in a single life is provided by Blaise
Pascal. "Few men," said Landor, "have been graver than
Pascal; few have been wittier." Indeed, we must say, in spite of

[6] *Phaedo*, 115C. Trans. by Hugh Tredennick (Penguin Classics, 154).
[7] Samuel Taylor Coleridge, *Writings on Shakespeare*, ed. by Terence Hawkes
(New York: G. P. Putnam's Sons, 1959), p. 158.

ır admiration for Bergson's famous essay on laughter, that the philosopher was wrong in saying that laughter is usually accompanied by an absence of feeling. "Indifference," he wrote, "is its natural environment, for laughter has no greater foe than emotion."[8] The probability is that Bergson would not have arrived at this conclusion if he had included the laughter of Christ in his researches.

Our logical mistake, which arises when we suppose that the assertion of Christ's sadness necessitates a denial of His humor, is the result of a superficial and therefore false application of the law of noncontradiction. This law, which is basic to all rational thinking, received its classic expression in Aristotle's *Metaphysics* (Book Gamma). It states that a thing cannot both be and not be at the same time and in the same sense. Only a confused mind could hold both that the earth is more than six thousand years old and that it is *not* more than six thousand years old. We do not know, in advance, which one of two contradictory propositions is erroneous, but we know that *one* of them is. All of this is extremely important, since, unless such a logical law is accepted, there cannot be any rational discussion between human beings. There is no point in trying to be intellectually honest if inconsistency is acceptable. But once we accept the Aristotelian law we need to be very careful about claiming that propositions are contradictory when they are not. Contrariety and contradiction are vastly different conceptions. For example, there is a great contrast between the proposition "All men are wise" and the contrary proposition "No men are wise." Far from being contradictory, these may both be false and, as a matter of fact, *are* both false. In a slightly different logical context it can be said of laughter and tears that, though they are extremely different, they are mutually compatible, providing we consider a person's

---

[8] *Comedy*, being *An Essay on Comedy* by George Meredith and *Laughter* by Henri Bergson, Introduction and Appendix by Wylie Sypher (Garden City, N. Y.: Doubleday Anchor Books, 1956), p. 63.

total character. The affirmation of one does not entail the denial of the other, for they are not contradictories.

Even our own experience in our own day should be sufficient to make us realize that laughter and a sense of concern are not really antithetical. We soon learn that we get better stories at a religious conference than we get anywhere else, and it is a commonplace that many Christian leaders are superlative tellers of humorous anecdotes. The late Rufus M. Jones was an example of this truth, but he did not stand alone. "The opposite of joy," says Leslie Weatherhead, "is not sorrow. It is unbelief."[9] It is not really surprising, therefore, that the Christian should laugh and sing; after all he has a great deal to laugh about. He understands, with George Fox, that, though there is an ocean of darkness and death, there is also an ocean of light and love which flows over the ocean of darkness.

Full recognition of Christ's humor has been surprisingly rare. In many of the standard efforts to write the Life of Christ there is no mention of humor at all, and when there is any, it is usually confined to a hint or two. Frequently, there is not one suggestion that He ever spoke other than seriously. It is to Renan's credit that he sensed the existence of the humorous element in the Gospels and called it striking, though he did not develop his insight in detail. Tennyson, in pointing out the paradox that humor is generally most fruitful in the most solemn spirits, said, "You will even find it in the Gospel of Christ." In several authors of the twentieth century we find a passing reference to the humorous side of Christ's teaching, though without development, in most cases. Characteristic is the reference of Harry Emerson Fosdick, "He never jests as Socrates does, but He often lets the ripple of a happy breeze play over the surface of His mighty deep."[10]

[9] Leslie Weatherhead, *This is the Victory* (Nashville: Abingdon Press, 1941), p. 171.
[10] Harry Emerson Fosdick, *The Manhood of the Master* (New York: The Association Press, 1958), p. 16.

Many readers who have come to maturity in the present centu₁y owe their first recognition of Christ's humor to a brilliant English scholar, T. R. Glover, who, during the dark days of the First World War, published *The Jesus of History*.[11] Glover gave especial attention to the subject in some very striking pages of Chapter III, "The Man and His Mind." He recognized fully that it is only familiarity that has blinded us "to the gaiety and playfulness that light up his lessons."[12] One of the best passages in this remarkable book is the following:

A more elaborate and amusing episode is that of the Pharisees' drinking operations. We are shown the man polishing his cup, elaborately and carefully; for he lays great importance on the cleanness of his cup; but he forgets to clean the inside. Most people drink from the inside, but the Pharisee forgot it, dirty as it was, and left it untouched. Then he sets about straining what he is going to drink—another elaborate process, and the series of sensations, as the long hairy neck slid down the throat of the Pharisee—all that amplitude of loose-hung anatomy—the hump—two humps—both of them slid down—and he never noticed—and the legs—all of them—with whole outfit of knees and big padded feet. The Pharisee swallowed a camel and never noticed it. (Matt. xxiii, 24, 25.) It is the mixture of sheer realism with absurdity that makes the irony and gives it its force. Did no one smile as the story was told? Did no one see the scene pictured with his own mind's eye—no one grasp the humor and the irony with delight? Could any one, on the other hand, forget it? A modern teacher would have said, in our jargon, that the Pharisee had no sense of proportion—and no one would have thought the remark worth remembering.[13]

Glover showed that Christ was no Stoic, much as Chesterton showed that the understanding Christian is no Epicurean. It is quite possible that the face of Marcus Aurelius never

[11] New York: The Association Press, 1917.
[12] *Ibid.*, p. 47.
[13] *Ibid.*, pp. 47-48.

changed, for his philosophy advocated superiority to emotion, but with Christ we are in another kind of world. His look showed anger and sorrow "at their obstinate stupidity" (Mark 3:5, N.E.B.). He was "moved with compassion" and He must have laughed, for those who tell jokes usually do.

Though a few books include references to the humor of Christ,[14] the most original and perceptive of modern writings on the subject is not in a book at all, but appeared in a most unlikely place, *The American Mercury*. The essay is by L. M. Hussey, and is called "The Wit of the Carpenter."[15] For some reason this has attracted very little scholarly attention and is seldom listed in bibliographies, even though it is executed with skill.

It is Hussey's hypothesis that the original followers of Christ reported what they did not appreciate or even understand, but that the speech was so pithy and so memorable that they found it easy to retain it and to convey it to those who eventually did the writing. Sober prose, as everyone knows, is hard to memorize or to repeat with any accuracy, whereas poetry, or the scintillating epigram, can be repeated with remarkable ease and faithfulness. The rough fisherman laughed and missed some of the nuances of the wit, but passed the wit on even more accurately for that reason. Referring to the persons who were Christ's first listeners, Hussey says, "I mean that by virtue of their naïveté they were literal-minded men—consequently of the sort to remember what they heard verbatim, and, unconscious of humorous implications, to set down their Teacher's sayings with almost mechanical verbal accuracy."[16] Literal

---

[14] *Laughter in the Bible* by Gary Webster (St. Louis: Bethany Press, 1960) has one chapter called "Jesus' Use of Humor." There is a short article on "Humor" in *The Interpreter's Dictionary of the Bible*, Vol. II, pp. 660-62. Other books are Dudley Zuver, *Salvation by Laughter* (New York: Harper & Brothers, 1933), D. N. Morison, *The Humour of Christ* (London, 1931).

[15] *The American Mercury*, Vol. V., pp. 329-36.

[16] *Ibid.*, p. 329.

faithfulness, Hussey speculates, was made possible by epigrammatic pungency of speech, which fixed itself indelibly in the memories of essentially illiterate men.

There is no doubt that this hypothesis has much in its favor. Certainly the epigrams have a freshness about them that it is impossible to believe is the result of the work of editors. Furthermore, we can frequently note a marked difference between the words attributed to Jesus and the clumsy attempts at justification or explanation. We have abundant evidence that the disciples failed, in a number of instances, to understand their Master.

A vivid illustration of such evidence appears when Christ says, "Beware of the leaven of the Pharisees and the leaven of Herod." His reference to the twin dangers of the Right and the Left was too advanced for the disciples. We can glow in his flaming impatience.

And they discussed it with one another, saying, "We have no bread." And being aware of it, Jesus said to them, "Why do you discuss the fact that you have no bread? Do you not yet perceive or understand? Are your hearts hardened? Having eyes do you not see, and having ears do you not hear? And do you not remember? [Mark 8:16-18]

A worse example of the failure of the Apostles to understand is shown in their argument about which one of them should be greatest, an argument which occurred in the most inappropriate setting, that of the Last Supper. If we may judge by John's account, the misunderstanding was so great that Christ undertook to correct it, not primarily by words which appeared to be wasted, but rather by the visible demonstration of washing their feet. Another sad evidence of misunderstanding came during Christ's final earthly appearance when, in spite of all that He had taught, they showed that they still had political expectations and asked, "Lord, will you at this time restore the kingdom to Israel?" (Acts 1:6). The contrast, Hussey claims, between the original word of Jesus and the reaction of His hearers is often apparent, because the disciples "set about to torture a literal significance from phrases first coined to blast utterly a literal intent."

The writer who has done most, in the twentieth century, to overcome the misapprehension that Christianity is a religion of sorrow and only of sorrow, is G. K. Chesterton. The paradox of the fundamental sadness of all Epicureanism was one of Chesterton's most revealing insights. Readers took notice when he showed them, in *Heretics*, the enormous contrast between the gay spirit of the early Christian and the pensiveness of an Omar Khayyám. People who had been complaining about Puritanism suddenly found that the shoe had been placed on the other foot. It was not hard for Chesterton to show that the characteristic man of classical antiquity was less boisterous than the Christian. The characteristic pagan philosopher believed in moderation, but the word does not appear in the New Testament, provided it is accurately translated. Even the most gifted of all the students of Socrates felt impelled, in his final work of maturity (a work in which the disturbing character of Socrates does not appear in the dialogue) to warn against both immoderate laughter and immoderate tears. The Athenian Stranger explains that "there must be restraint of unseasonable laughter and tears and each of us must urge his fellow to consult decorum by utter concealment of all excess of joy or grief, whether the breeze of fortune is set fair, or, by a shift of circumstance, the fortunes of an enterprise are confronted by a mountain of difficulty."[17]

The reader can see that the mood of the aged Plato, whatever his greatness, is far removed from the mood of Christ, which could include hot anger and great rejoicing. This con-

[17] *Laws*, V. 732C by A. E. Taylor, *The Collected Dialogues of Plato* (Bollingen Series LXXI, Pantheon Books, 1961).

trast between the best of the classical spirit and the best of Christianity gave G. K. Chesterton his opportunity to elaborate a paradox and thus to challenge a generally accepted opinion. Though Chesterton shocked many of his contemporaries by showing, in *Heretics*, that Christianity is fundamentally a religion of joy, markedly in contrast to the melancholy mood of Omar Khayyám, it was in *Orthodoxy* that he completed his case. He tells us:

It is said that Paganism is a religion of joy and Christianity of sorrow; it would be just as easy to prove that Paganism is pure sorrow and Christianity pure joy. Such conflicts mean nothing and lead nowhere. Everything human must have in it both joy and sorrow; the only matter of interest is the manner in which the two things are balanced or divided. And the really interesting thing is this, that the pagan was (in the main) happier and happier as he approached the earth, but sadder and sadder as he approached the heavens.[18]

Chesterton is quite ready to concede that the men and women of the pagan civilizations could be gay about *some* things. Indeed, this is obvious. It is impressive, for example, to see how Aristophanes could make people smile about such important subjects as science and war. But Chesterton contends that it took something like the Gospel to make poor men experience "cosmic contentment." Men, who had come to know Christ, might be sad about the little things, but were tumultuously gay about the big things. "Giotto lived in a gloomier town than Euripides, but he lived in a gayer universe." Christianity fits man's deepest need because it makes him concentrate on joys which do not pass away, rather than on the inevitable grief which is superficial. The climax of Chesterton's great book is memorable:

[18] Chesterton, *Orthodoxy* (New York: Dodd, Mead & Co., 1927), pp. 294-95.

And as I close this chaotic volume I open again the strange small book from which all Christianity came; and I am again haunted by a kind of confirmation. The tremendous figure which fills the Gospels towers in this respect, as in every other above all the thinkers who ever thought themselves tall. His pathos was natural, almost casual. The Stoics, ancient and modern, were proud of concealing their tears. He never concealed His tears; He showed them plainly on His open face at any daily sight, such as the far sight of His native city. Yet He concealed something. Solemn supermen and imperial diplomatists are proud of restraining their anger. He never restrained His anger. He flung furniture down the front steps of the Temple, and asked men how they expected to escape the damnation of Hell. Yet He restrained something. . . . There was something that He covered constantly by abrupt silence or impetuous isolation. There was some one thing that was too great for God to show us when He walked upon our earth; and I have sometimes fancied that it was his mirth.[19]

What is really strange about Chesterton, at this point, is his failure to see the open evidence of the humor of Christ, when he saw so much of it in the movement which stems from Him. Some of Christ's humor may have ben "covered," but it is not true to say that all of it was of the hidden variety. Chesterton has put us greatly in his debt because of the way in which he has helped to restore a balance, but, if the evidence assembled in this book is correctly interpreted, we have to conclude that he did not go far enough.

The conception of Christianity in which compassion and joy were equally at home was given brilliant expression, a generation ago, in a pamphlet, published by the Epworth Press, called *God in Everything*. In this, Parson John writes to Miriam Gray,

Many of the religious people that I know, when they talk of religion, have a bedside manner and walk about in felt slippers. And if they speak of God they always tidy themselves first. But

[19] *Ibid.*, pp. 298-99.

you go in and out of all the rooms in God's house as though you were quite at home. You open the doors without knocking, and you hum on the stairs, and it isn't always hymns either. My aunt thinks you are not quite reverent; but, then, she can keep felt slippers on her mind without any trouble.

Any alleged Christianity which fails to express itself in gaiety, at some point, is clearly spurious. The Christian is gay, not because he is blind to injustice and suffering, but because he is convinced that these, in the light of the divine sovereignty, are never *ultimate*. He is convinced that the unshakable purpose is the divine rule in all things, whether of heaven or earth (Eph. 1:10). Though he can be sad, and often is perplexed, he is never really worried. The well-known humor of the Christian is not a way of denying the tears, but rather a way of affirming something which is deeper than tears.

The consequences of Christ's rejection of the dismal are great, not only for common life, but also for theology. If Christ laughed a great deal, as the evidence shows, and if He is what He claimed to be, we cannot avoid the logical conclusion that there is laughter and gaiety in the heart of God. The deepest conviction of all Christian theology is the affirmation that the God of all the world is like Jesus Christ. Because the logical development is from the relatively known to the relatively unknown, the procedure is not from God to Christ, but from Christ to God. If we take this seriously we conclude that God cannot be cruel, or self-centered or vindictive, or even lacking in humor.

CHAPTER II

❧

The Universality of Christ's Humor

> Humor is always a concealed pair.
> *Søren Kierkegaard*

DIFFERENT RACES or nations tend to believe that they exhibit slightly different kinds of humor and each seems to suppose that it is especially gifted in this important regard. Thus William Hazlitt sought to explain why the English crop of humor was so luxuriant. "Now it appears to me," he wrote, "that the English are (or were) just at the mean point between intelligence and obtuseness, which must produce the most abundant and happiest crop of humor. . . . The ludicrous takes hold of the English imagination, and clings to it with all its ramifications."[1]

It is quite possible that each national claim to a particular character of humor is a matter of self-delusion. In any case, Christ, with His Hebrew heritage, seems to meet all of the qualifications which the perceptive Hazlitt lays down for English wit. Possibly Christ's humor was one mark of His universality. There was, of course, some Hebrew humor, which has been the subject of careful study in our time,[2] but an

---

[1] William Hazlitt, "Merry England," *Lectures on the English Comic Writers* (Everyman Edition), p. 191.
[2] See T. W. Manson, *The Teaching of Jesus* (New York: Cambridge Uni-

understanding of it adds very little that is needed for an appreciation of Christ's humor.

It might be supposed that an appreciation of Christ's humor would be severely handicapped by the language barrier. Presumably He spoke in Aramaic, while the New Testament was written in Greek, and most of us now read it in a contemporary tongue. As a matter of fact, however, this barrier is by no means insurmountable. Undoubtedly we miss a great deal of the word play which was so attractive to the ancients. Such word play, called *paronomasia*, of which the pun is one variety, is profusely employed in the Old Testament,[3] but it is obvious that most of Christ's humor was of a deeper variety than this. Some word play is humorous and some is not, and it, of course, loses more in translation than does any other form of humor. Puns, we know, are hard to carry over from one language to another. We lose in translation some of the intended wit, but it does not follow that we miss the deeper humor when it appears, for Christ's characteristic humor depends, for the most part, upon a combination of ideas rather than upon a combination of words. This is why the particular language, be it Aramaic or some other, makes no crucial difference. The swallowing of the camel is funny in any language. Careful studies of Jewish life may help, but acquaintance with them is not really necessary.

In our emphasis upon cultural history we are likely to suppose that understanding is denied those of a later age, but this is not always true. Coleridge was helping us over a prejudice in this connection when he wrote, "I believe Shakespeare was not a whit more intelligible in his own day than

---

versity Press, 1935), for a study of the Old Testament background, particularly in regard to parables.

[3] Dissertations on paronomasia have been produced at Yale University, at Johns Hopkins University and at the University of Chicago. See E. Russell, *Paronomasia and Kindred Phenomena in the New Testament* (Chicago: University of Chicago Press, 1920).

he is now to an educated man, except for a few local allusions of no consequence."[4]

It has been said many times that man is the only animal who laughs, and this is true, for the laughter of other creatures is only apparent, but not one claims to understand fully what laughter means. It is connected, of course, with our gift of self-consciousness. We are not only conscious of others but also of our consciousness of others and even of our consciousness of ourselves. Most philosophers, who have delved deeply into the subject, have been forced to the conclusion that man's tendency to laugh is too complex to be reduced to any single explanation. Bergson's essay on "Laughter" is profound and possibly the best ever written, but even he must have been dissatisfied at the end. He says some perceptive things, especially in the insistence that humor "does not exist outside the pale of what is strictly human," and that "laughter appears to stand in need of an echo," but the great essay seems to break off suddenly, and the reader is aware that there is no fundamental success in the search. We can agree with Wylie Sypher when he concludes, in his perceptive essay based on the work of Meredith and Bergson, that "we do not really know what laughter is or what causes it."[5]

Christ was demonstrating one of the universal elements of His humor when He served the cause of true religion by exposing the pompous person whose profession far exceeds his practice. Humor is not hostile to religion, but it is hostile, as Meredith observed, "to the priestly element when that, by baleful swelling, transcends and overlaps the bounds of its office."[6] Vanity is a great weakness of mankind in general, but it seems especially ludicrous when it appears among the pro-

---

[4] Coleridge, *Writings on Shakespeare*, ed. by Terence Hawkes (New York: G. P. Putnam's Sons, 1959), p. 106.
[5] Wylie Sypher, Appendix to *Comedy, op. cit.*, p. 201.
[6] *Ibid.*, p. 49.

fessionally religious. The contradiction between man's humility before God and his strutting before men is a perfect opening for ridicule, and Jesus employed it to perfection in the twenty-third chapter of Matthew's Gospel.

Solemnity in professions is highly vulnerable. This is why there is so much about pretentious physicians in French comedy. While tragedy deals primarily with the individual, says Bergson, comedy finds its opportunity in classes and groups. All of the ancient Quaker jokes, which are so numerous and, on the whole, so truly funny, turn on the inherent inconsistency which is demonstrated by a crack in the supposed armor of external righteousness. The eighteenth-century Quaker, with his plain garb and his "Thee" and "Thou," was especially vulnerable, as Dr. Johnson detected in one of his famous sallies, preserved for us by Mrs. Piozzi. "Sir," he said, "a man who cannot get to heaven in a green coat, will not find his way thither sooner in a gray one."[7]

Rigidity and pretension are what ordinary humans tend to eye with suspicion. This is why the common people apparently rejoiced in Christ's humorous attacks on the Pharisaic party. "A flexible vice," said Bergson, "may not be so easy to ridicule as a rigid virtue." Aristophanes found it easy to make people laugh at the Sophists, partly because people were delighted to see something wrong in a class which claimed so much for itself. The Sophists were vain about their skill in teaching, as the Jerusalem scribes were vain about their legal learning. If it were not for the medicine of created laughter, there would be no adequate antidote to pride and vanity among men. God has created us with a self-consciousness which makes conceit possible, but He has also made us able to laugh and thus to provide a balance to our danger. Though Bergson said many profound things on this subject, perhaps the most

[7] Hester Piozzi, *Anecdotes of Doctor Samuel Johnson*, Number 57.

profound of all was along this line. "It might be said," he wrote, "that the specific remedy for vanity is laughter, and that the one failing that is essentially laughable is vanity."[8]

The danger of this appropriate cure is that it may hurt too much, at the same time that it heals. But it does not hurt so much if the one who laughs has enough insight and objectivity to laugh at himself while he also laughs at others. The only kind of laughter which can be redemptive is that which goes beyond scorn to recognition of a common predicament. If laughter were all that Thomas Hobbes thought it was, it would be almost wholly vicious. It is, he thought, the "sudden glory" which arises from our feeling of superiority whenever we see ourselves triumphantly secure while others stumble. Unless this pose of superiority can be transcended, laughter is a cruel vice. But it can be transcended, and Ernst Cassirer has told us how. "We live," he says, in this restricted world, but we are no longer imprisoned by it. . . . Scorn is dissolved into laughter and laughter is liberation."[9] Laughter is not cruelly humiliating, provided we are all humiliated together.

THE CHILD SPIRIT

The recognition that Christ understood and demonstrated humor helps us to see a greater profundity in the dictum that it is impossible to enter the Kingdom except as we become little children (Mark 10:15). The incident mentioned in the Preface is a case in point, but only a few, like Kierkegaard, have seen it. The child laughs because he has not yet been brainwashed and thereby blinded to the truly amusing. The serious Dane understood the connection between childlikeness and humor, and thereby gave us a new understanding of how the becoming as a little child is one of the necessary

[8] *Comedy, op cit.,* p. 173.
[9] Cassirer *Essay on Man* (New Haven: Yale University Press, 1944), p. 192.

conditions of entrance into the Kingdom. "The humorous effect," he wrote in *Concluding Unscientific Postscript*, "is produced by letting the childlike trait reflect itself in the consciousness of totality." The normal child laughs a great deal, partly because his mind is not yet accustomed to the surprising paradoxes of reality. The humorist is one who is still partly a child in that he "possesses the childlike quality, but is not possessed by it." He sees the grotesque as grotesque because, by God's grace, he has been saved from the sad fate of taking it for granted. It is part of the greatness of Kierkegaard that he understood the theory of the significance of the childlike; it is part of the greatness of Jesus Christ that he *demonstrated* it.

Most of the standard efforts to portray Christ's physical likeness make him seem mature, and sometimes far too old for one whose earthly life did not extend much beyond thirty years. That He was mature, especially in His insight into the motives and temptations of men, we cannot doubt, but this is only one side of the truth. The other side is the glorification of what it is to be a child. Grateful readers of Sir Arthur Quiller-Couch may remember a passage in which the Cambridge lecturer combined his judgment about literature with the childlike aspect of Christ's teaching.

I preach to you that the base of all Literature, of all Poetry, of all Theology, is one, and stands on one rock: *the very highest Universal Truth is something so simple that a child may understand it.* This surely was in Jesus' mind when He said, "I thank thee, O Father, Lord of heaven and earth, because thou hast hid these things from the wise and prudent, and hast revealed them unto babes."[10]

The recognition of the connection between the humorous and the childlike is one of the many features of Kierkegaard's

[10] Sir Arthur Quiller-Couch, *On the Art of Reading* (New York: Cambridge University Press, 1953), p. 53.

philosophical and religious genius. As Kierkegaard's faithful readers have learned to expect, he stated his insight paradoxically. Humor, he taught, is a reflection of the childlike, but it is not inconsistent with true maturity. This gives us both lightness and sadness at once. "For the sadness in legitimate humor consists in the fact that honestly and without deceit it reflects in a purely human way upon what it is to be a child."[11] We cannot truly laugh unless, in some sense, we become as children, but only the mature person, like Francis Thompson, knows what it is to be a child. Thompson, because he knew, as an adult, how dull grown men and women can become, in their insensitivity to the surrounding wonder, could say, in his poetry, that when we seek his location in heaven, we should look in the nursery area.

> For if in Eden as on earth are we,
> I sure shall keep a younger company.

The balance between the childlike and the mature in Christ's life is really amazing. It is not a mere compromise in the middle, a mean of exclusion, but rather a mean of comprehension. On the one hand, He can rejoice unconditionally in the Father's care, without which not a sparrow falls, but, on the other hand, He can see through the pretensions of men and women, particularly their religious pretensions. Because, in Christ, there was the acme of both the childlike and the mature, humor was inevitable. Humor appears where the two worlds meet.

PARADOX

Kierkegaard, in his careful inquiry, was not surprised at the connection which exists between deep religious experience and humor. He believed that the religious individual

[11] Kierkegaard, *op. cit.*, p. 533.

discovers the comical in the largest measure, partly because, in religion, men are acutely conscious of sharp inconsistencies. Every inconsistency, once it is really made manifest, is potentially humorous. The German philosopher, Schopenhauer, considered this to be the central feature in all laughter. Laughter, he thought, is "the sudden perception of incongruity" between our ideals and the actualities that are before us.

The employment of paradox arises from the recognition that our world is too complex to be represented, adequately, by reference to a single aspect of it. Sometimes the complexity is so great that we have to use propositions which appear to be contradictory, though they cannot be absolutely so, if truth is one. There is a sense in which Christ came to bring peace, but there is another sense in which He came to bring a sword, and we must try to understand both of these if we are to begin to grasp the truth.

Though we do not know the ultimate secret of laughter, even laughter at ourselves, we can see that contradiction, or at least *apparent* contradiction, has something to do with it. Man, whatever else he is, is a double creature, who is in one sense an animal, but in another sense is not one, for no animal recognizes his animality. Man can see the difference, always, between what he is and what he ought to be, between the positivistic fact and the ethical norm. Every man is therefore something of a hypocrite, because no one lives up to his pretensions, yet we realize that we should be even more degraded if we were wholly without such pretensions. The fact that we are hypocrites is the source of most of our hope and also the source of most of our anguish. But the hypocrite is always vulnerable to ridicule! This is why it is easy for us to understand the meaning of Christ's wit when He directs His barbs at the religious. He is talking to us! But the purpose of all of the Gospel, even of its jokes, is redemption.

We call Kierkegaard the father of existentialism partly because he held that wherever there is life there is paradox, but he also recognized that wherever there is paradox the comic element is present, at least potentially. The essence of paradox is the recognition of a connection, often between apparent opposites, a connection which makes possible both humor and poetry. The similiarity which exists between poetry and humor may easily be missed, but a man of the caliber of Robert Frost can make us see it.

Every joke, like every poem, Frost contended, is based on an idea and the connection between the two forms of human expression is close and real. "Then you have to know," said Frost, "what an *idea* is, in a joke or in a poem. You have to know how to make a point, to point up an idea."[12] In either the poetry or the joke, in contrast to sober prose, the idea can be conveyed with sharpness and with distilled brevity.[13] The long-drawn anecdote, as everyone knows, becomes almost unbearably boring, and consequently ceases to be funny.

What is supremely important, in considering the mysterious area which lies between poetry and prose, is to know what an idea is. As we reflect carefully, we realize that it is never single; *it always involves a connection*. Therefore we can appreciate the pithy wisdom of Aristotle when he said, "Only connect." The profundity lies in combining two realities which have a connecting point, but are not usually associated in our commonplace thought. The combination brings surprise and consequent delight. "I have often tried," wrote Robert Frost, "to tell what an idea is. It is a feat of association. That's one of my definitions for it. It reaches its height in a good metaphor. Many metaphors are unemotional. Every philosopher has one big metaphor in him. That is all he has."

That the aged Frost was far on the road to understanding

[12] "Between Prose and Verse," in *The Atlantic Monthly*, January, 1962, p. 51.

[13] Bergson corroborates Frost's insight by saying, "In every wit there is something of a poet—just as in every good reader there is the making of an actor." (In Sypher, *op. cit.*, p. 129.)

the mystery of humor we cannot doubt, and we are grateful for what he revealed. What is bound to occur to one who is familiar with the Gospels is that the humor of Christ is based largely on what Frost stresses, i.e., on connections which are genuine, but which ordinary men do not recognize without help. Christ seems to have noted these connections everywhere, starting with the most common experiences of ordinary life. His metaphors concern the plow, the seed, the yoke, the salt, the light, the leaven, the door, the coin, the jewel, the fire, and many more. Each one is placed in an association which we can never forget but which we did not discover with our own unaided powers. Some of these are humorous and some are not, but it is reasonable to suppose that they represent only a few of Christ's flashing insights. After all, an exceedingly small portion of His total life is recorded in the Gospels. If, as it is reasonable to conclude, most of His words are forever lost, our loss is great indeed.

Even the unhumorous metaphors constitute a challenge to the commonplace associations. The conception of baptism by fire, which Christ took over from John and gave emphasis (Luke 12:49, 50), is so violent that even the most confirmed literalist would never attempt to practice it. The famous metaphor of Christ's Yoke was striking, in the first instance, precisely because it *reversed* all familiar associations. When Christ said, "Take my yoke upon you" (Matt. 11:29), He was accepting boldly the very instrument which was looked upon by Isaiah and Jeremiah as hateful (Isa. 58:6-9, Jer. 28:10-14). The yoke was well known, but was universally regarded, before Christ, as something to be avoided. The change wrought by Christ in the meaning of the metaphor was so revolutionary that, far from avoiding it, early Christians could adopt it and call one another Yokefellows (Phil. 4:3).

What Christ said was true, but it was never a truism. The escape from truism came by the consistent employment of paradox in which there is always a hint of the laughable. For example, the paradox of the blind leading the blind is absurdity carried as far as it can go (Luke 6:39). It is clear that, though Christ's use of paradox was appreciated by the perceptive, it was missed by the unhumorous and the literal-minded. An illustration of the latter response is the literalistic question of Nicodemus when faced with the radical metaphor of new birth. Such use of paradox became a means of selection among hearers, with the consequence that many did not really hear, though there was nothing wrong with their physical ears. This fact provided the setting for the pungent saying, "Take heed what you hear" (Mark 4:24). Unjust as it sounds, it is a fact, at least in the realm of understanding, that the rich get richer and the poor get poorer (Mark 4:25).

Christ's use of paradox is dazzling. The entire process of finding similarity in apparent difference, which makes parable possible, is deeply paradoxical. At first sight the different metaphors which Christ uses to explain the character of the new redemptive fellowship which He is establishing, particularly *salt, light,* and *leaven,* seem radically different, but, on closer examination, all mean the same thing. Each is a figure of *penetration,* and each fulfills its function only by spending or by losing itself. Thus the theme of the cross, i.e., of saving by losing, is far more pervasive of the Gospel than it at first appears to be. It is even the point of the acted parable of the breaking of bread during the last meal together. It is the ultimate of paradox. So moving was it to the restless mind of Dostoyevsky that he used the paradox as an epigraph for his final and greatest work of fiction, *The Brothers Karamazov.* At the beginning of the book are the words, "Verily, verily, I say unto you, except a corn of wheat fall into the ground and die, it abideth alone: but if it die it bringeth forth much fruit." (John 12:24, A.V.).

Only our excessive familiarity with the words which Matthew places at the beginning of the Sermon on the Mount can make us unaware of how close the individual Beatitudes come to absolute self-contradiction. It is good, we are told, to be meek and to mourn and to be reviled. In Luke's version (6:20-26) the paradox is even more sharp, because blessedness is said to come from actual *poverty*, rather than from poverty of spirit. Furthermore, the negative aspect is added. It is not really fortunate, we learn, to be rich or to be well fed or to be popular. The paradox lies in the fact that the standard view is challenged and challenged in a way that is easily remembered. The Beatitudes are not humorous, but they provide a setting in which it is possible for the gay sally to appear. A great difference between the Synoptics and the Fourth Gospel is the fact that John preserves nothing remotely similar to the Beatitudes, and consequently little humor.

One of the reasons for concluding that the Synoptics preserve a more faithful record of Christ's words is that so many of the words reported by them, in contrast to those found in John, are of the kind that men *can* remember. Even the illiterate listener could hardly forget what he had heard if the words were "blessed are you that weep now, for you shall laugh," whereas the long disquisitions found in John could not be remembered verbatim by *anybody*. "In this matter," wrote Donald Hankey, "we are bound to doubt John, because the sermons which he puts into the mouth of Jesus are so long and deep that they could not have been remembered for all those years after only being heard once."[14] Hankey recognizes, of course, that John keeps a few vivid and memorable sentences and holds that, in some respects, the authenticity of John's account is even greater than is that of any of the Synoptics. Dostoyevsky's epigraph is a case in point.

Paradox is necessary for the emergence of humor, but it

[14] Donald Hankey, *The Lord of All Good Life* (London: Longmans, Green and Company, 1918), p. 170.

is not sufficient. We recognize this truth when we note that there is much paradox that is not even slightly humorous.[15] The paradox which Dostoyevsky selected for his epigraph is a violent one, but not amusing in the faintest degree. Why is some paradox funny and some not? We may as well realize that this is an unanswered question and one which is not likely to receive an adequate answer. We know a little. We know that a paradox is more likely to arouse laughter if it exposes presumption or cuts down to size those who take themselves overseriously. We know that a paradox is more humorous if it does not involve real tragedy or unmerited suffering. We know that it is easier to laugh if the situation presented in the joke is slightly remote in time or in place or in condition. We laugh at the cartoon showing two men in prison with one saying, "There is no place for the little man in crime any more," partly because most of us are not behind bars. Yet there are situations, and these are among the noblest of all, in which the humorous and the tragic are parts of one picture. Perhaps there is no finer evidence of this possibility than that provided by Donald Hankey when he wrote from the trenches in the First World War. Without intending to do so, Hankey produced a devotional classic. It is in this classic that Hankey defined "true religion" as "betting one's life that there is a God."[16] In the days immediately preceding his death in action on the Western Front on October 26, 1916, Donald Hankey created some of the finest prose of the twentieth century. The key passage, which bears on the theme of this

[15] A good example of modern paradox, not unlike that used by Christ, is in Robert Frost's "Mending Wall." Though the final line words are "Good fences make good neighbors," the opening words are "Something there is that doesn't love a wall." Both sides of the paradox are needed to tell the truth. This is like Christ's balancing statements, "My peace I leave with you" and "Do not suppose I came to bring peace."

[16] Donald Hankey, *A Student in Arms* (New York: E. P. Dutton and Company, 1917), p. 190.

book, and which refers to the gay spirit with which the men of Kitchener's army faced death, is as follows:

Their spirits effervesced. Their wits sparkled. Hunger and thirst could not depress them. Rain could not damp them. Cold could not chill them. Every hardship became a joke. They did not endure hardship, they derided it. And somehow it seemed at the moment as if derision was all that hardship existed for! Never was such a triumph of spirit over matter. As for death, it was, in a way, the greatest joke of all. In a way, for if it was another fellow that was hit, it was an occasion for tenderness and grief. But if one of them was hit, O Death, where is thy sting? O Grave, where is thy victory? Portentous, solemn Death, you looked a fool when you tackled one of them! Life? They did not value life! They had never been able to make much of a fist of it. But if they lived amiss they died gloriously, with a smile for the pain and the dread of it. What else had they been born for? It was their chance. With a gay heart they gave their greatest gift, and with a smile to think that after all they had anything to give which was of value. One by one Death challenged them. One by one they smiled in his grim visage, and refused to be dismayed. They had been lost, but they had found the path that led them home; and when at last they laid their lives at the feet of the Good Shepherd, what could they do but smile?[17]

In Hankey's expressions we get what is virtually a commentary on the wit and humor of the Gospel, and we see the reason for it. Christ's humor is a demonstration of what The Student in Arms was talking about.

THE PREPOSTEROUS

Of all the mistakes which we make in regard to the humor of Christ, perhaps the worst mistake is our failure, or our unwillingness, to recognize that Christ used deliberately pre-

[17] *Ibid.*, pp. 23-25.

posterous statements to get His point across. When we take a deliberately preposterous statement and, from a false sense of piety, try to force some literal truth out of it, the result is often grotesque. The playful, when interpreted with humorless seriousness, becomes merely ridiculous. An excellent illustration of this is a frequent handling of the gigantic dictum about the rich man and the needle's eye, an elaborate figure which appears in identical form in all three of the Synoptics. "It is easier," said Jesus, "for a camel to go through the eye of a needle than for a rich man to enter the kingdom of God" (Mark 10:25). This categorical statement, given with no qualifications whatever, follows, in all three accounts, the story of a wealthy man who came to Jesus to ask seriously how he might have eternal life. He claimed to have kept the standard commandments, but he went away sorrowfully when told that, at least in his case, it would be necessary to divest himself of all of his possessions.

We are informed that Christ's hearers were greatly astonished, and well they might have been, if they took the dictum literally, as they apparently did. Taken literally, of course, the necessary conclusion is that no one who is not in absolute poverty can enter the Kingdom, because most people have some riches, and it is impossible for a body as large as that of a camel, hump and all, to go through an aperture as small as the eye of a needle. For humorous purposes this is evidently the same camel swallowed by the Pharisee when he carefully rejected the gnat. That the listeners failed to see the epigram about the needle's eye as a violent metaphor is shown by their question, "Then who can be saved?" (Mark 10:26).

By making the statement in such an exaggerated form, termed by Chesterton the *giantesque*, Christ made sure that it was memorable, whereas a prosy, qualified statement would certainly have been forgotten. The device is mirrored in our conventional Texas story, which no one believes literally, but which everyone remembers. Christ made his point, so that millions remember it today, though the first hearers misunderstood and kept it accurately only because it was so bizarre.

We need not be astonished if the fishermen failed to see Christ's humor about the needle's eye, but it is truly shocking to find that many contemporary Christians continue to make the same mistake, yet make it in a more elaborate way. Because they cannot bear the bold figure of the patently impossible, they say that Jesus did not really mean by the eye of a needle that through which people put thread for sewing. He meant, they say, a gate in Jerusalem which was so low that a camel could wriggle through it only with extreme difficulty, and even then without his load, which had to be removed if passage was to be accomplished. Thus, many moderns believe, they save the words of Christ from appearing preposterous. What they miss, by this devious explanation, in contradistinction to the plain sense, is that there is good reason to suppose that Christ *meant* His words to sound preposterous. We spoil the figure, and lose all the robustness, when we tone it down. Christ had a revolutionary message to give and He knew that He could not make Himself understood by speaking mildly. He said that, following John, "the good news of the kingdom of God is preached, and every one enters it violently" (Luke 16:16). We do not know all that He meant by "violently," but we do know that there was an element of "violence" in His speech, a feature which comes through to us today even after the toning down on the part of the reporters.

Christ's use of deliberate exaggeration is evident at many points in the Gospel record. One of the best illustrations of gay deliberate overstatement is found in the parable of the debtors, which only Matthew has preserved (Matt. 18:23-35). The gross inconsistency of the man who was forgiven a large debt and then refused to forgive a small one is pointed up by the contrast in amounts. Dr. Phillips makes the contrast vivid by his translation, mentioning, on the one hand, "millions of pounds," and, on the other, "a few shillings." This appears to be allied to the joke, already mentioned, concerning the log in the eye of the beholder and the speck in the eye of his neighbor.

Christ seems to employ exactly that amount of shock which is necessary to make people break through their deeply in-grained obtuseness. In some cases only the extreme form will suffice. An illustration of this is the figure of the dead under-taker. A would-be follower seeks to excuse himself for what seems to us a justifiable reason: he has to bury his father. Jesus, apparently tired of excuses, blurts out, "Leave the dead to bury their own dead; but as for you, go and proclaim the kingdom of God" (Luke 9:60). Here Luke states the paradox more fully than does Matthew, but both include the central assertion. A manifest impossibility is advised, as a clear means of making a point, where a milder figure would not have been as successful. When Christ said not to cast pearls before swine (Matt. 7:6), He was employing the patently absurd to make His point.[18] In contrast to the sentimentality, which would advise continued effort to win the habitually unresponsive, Christ tells us that we are not to waste precious words or time or effort on those who are chronically impervious. This is a laughable version of His advice to the Seventy when He said, "But whenever you enter a town and they do not receive you, go into its streets and say, 'Even the dust of your town that clings to our feet, we wipe off against you'" (Luke 10:10, 11). The fact that men never would, as a matter of fact, throw pearls to swine does not make the joke less funny, but renders it more so, for the preposterousness is the point. It has served well the purposes of generations of professors, when their students tend to become restless and unresponsive.

In one of Christ's few experiences with the priests, whom

[18] We must remember, of course, that the joke about casting what is precious before pigs was even more preposterous for a Jewish audience than it is for us. The rejection of pork was deep-seated in their consciousness.

He normally ignored, He said, in a sudden thrust, "the harlots go into the kingdom of God before you" (Matt. 21:31). It is doubtful if the priests smiled, but we do, provided we understand what He is saying. It is laughable to have the whores precede those who are professionally religious. And was there no smile when, with a superfluity of priests in existence, requiring them to serve in shifts at the Temple, Christ said on more than one occasion, "The harvest is plentiful, but the laborers are few" (Matt. 9:37 and Luke 10:2)? Part of the appeal in this approach lies in the quick change from chaffing to deep seriousness. The paradoxical scarcity of laborers leads to a command to pray. Because Christ was always in His Father's house the transition from one room to another was easy.

What we require, for Christ's kind of humor, are two ingredients, *surprise* and *inevitability*. There is a connection which we do not expect, but which, nevertheless, seems absolutely valid when once it is presented. "First of all," said Robert Frost, "the coupling that moves you, that stirs you, is an association of two things you don't expect to see associated."[19] Frost was repeating, in essence, the insight of Søren Kierkegaard reflected in the epigraph of this chapter, "Humor is always a concealed pair."

We make a mistake if, in studying the Gospels, and watching for evidence of humor, we look only for that which brings full laughter. Frequently there is only a slight touch of humor, such as we find in the couplet,

> Seeing they do not see
> And hearing they do not hear. [Matt. 13:13]

Often the smile comes because Jesus reveals to us some of the absurdity of our own lives, where we need help to recognize it. A good illustration of this is in the sly question inserted in

[19] Frost, *Atlantic Monthly*, *op. cit.*, p. 52.

the parable of equal payment, "Why be jealous because I am kind?" (Matt. 20:15, N.E.B.). Suddenly, by this quick turn, the objection is made to appear as ridiculous as it really is. We see our own inconsistency in the story of the judge who would not help the mistreated widow because her cause was just, yet finally helped her because he got tired of being bothered. He found it easier to do the right thing than to be pestered forever (Luke 18:1-5)! This is likewise the point of the story (Luke 11:5-9) about the householder who would not arise and help because of neighborliness, yet capitulated to importunity.

It is very important to understand that the evident purpose of Christ's humor is to clarify and increase understanding, rather than to hurt. Perhaps some hurt is inevitable, especially when, as we shall see more fully in Chapter IV, human pride is rendered ridiculous, but the clear aim is something other than harm. Irony, which we shall consider in Chapter III, sometimes moves over into sarcasm, but the sarcastic thrust is not the major factor. Most of Christ's humor belongs to what Meredith calls "the laughter of comedy." It is not like satire which "is a blow in the back or the face," but "is impersonal and of unrivalled politeness, nearer a smile—often no more than a smile."[20] The satirist may work on a "storage of bile," but this seems utterly absent in the humor preserved in the Gospels. The attack may be strong, when the object is the Pharisaic spirit, but it is not an attack upon an individual Pharisee.

The humor of Christ does not employ all of the humorous forms known, though it employs many which are familiar to us in subsequent literature. Perhaps the chief difference between Christ's humor and ours today is revealed in the fact that, in our ordinary experience, we make abundant use of the humorous anecdote, for its own sake. The laugh for which

[20] *Comedy, op. cit.,* p. 47.

we strive is often the sole justification of the entire effort. We seek humor for humor's sake. There seems to be little or none of this in the recorded words of Christ, where the purpose is always the revelation of some facet of truth which would not otherwise be revealed. The humor of Christ is employed, it would appear, only because it is a means of calling attention to what would, without it, remain hidden or unappreciated. Truth, and truth alone, is the end.

CHAPTER III

❧ ❧

Christ's Use of Irony

> Dulness, insensible to the comic,
> has the privilege of arousing it.
> *George Meredith*

HUMOR, such as that employed by Christ, is akin to dialectic, in that it can lead to the unmasking of error and, thereby, the emergence of truth. The humorous thrust clears away confusion, somewhat as logical analysis does. We value Milton's great idea, in the *Areopagitica*, that Truth will be found more efficiently in unlimited debate, which is a kind of trial. Conflict can be a shedder of light and humorous banter is a form of conflict. Because man is not a creature to whom Truth is given directly and simply, it is something for which he must struggle. In the first propagation of the Gospel, humor was part of the struggle. "For such is the order of God's enlightening his church," wrote Milton, "to disperse and deal out by degrees his beam, so as our earthly eyes may best sustain it."[1] Only in an open society, the antithesis of one which lives with Spartan efficiency, is clarification by controversy possible, and often the finest form that such controversy can take is high comedy.

[1] John Milton, *Prose Selections* (New York: The Odyssey Press, 1947), p. 265.

The sensitive editor of the essays on humor by Meredith and Bergson tells us that "the comic spirit keeps us pure in mind by requiring that we regard ourselves skeptically." Laughter, we are well aware, can be a cruel weapon and sometimes men are deeply hurt, but this fact must not blind us to the correlative fact that laughter can, if taken aright, have a purgative effect, though not identical to the purgative effect which Aristotle attributed to great tragedy. "No society is in good health without laughing at itself quietly and privately; no character is sound without self-scrutiny, without turning inward to see where it may have overreached itself."[2] Humor is redemptive when it leads to comic self-discovery. Christ brings such self-discovery to men who will listen and who know that they are responsible for what they hear. The most valuable use we can make of the wit and humor of Christ is to think of ourselves as Pharisees, as we to some extent are, and thus allow the comic purification to take place. We hate to be laughed at by one another, but we do not mind being laughed at by Him.

Though Meredith did not mention Christ and His humor, the following remarkable passage, referring to the Comic Spirit, applies perfectly:

Men's future upon earth does not attract it; their honesty and shapeliness in the present does; and whenever they wax out of proportion, overblown, affected, pretentious, bombastical, hypocritical, pedantic, fantastically delicate; whenever it sees them self-deceived or hoodwinked, given to run riot in idolatries, drifting into vanities, congregating in absurdities, planning short-sightedly, plotting dementedly; whenever they are at variance with their professions, and violate the unwritten but perceptible laws binding them in consideration one to another; whenever they offend sound reason, fair justice; are false in humility or mined with conceit, individually, or in the bulk; the Spirit overhead will humanely

---

[2] Wylie Sypher, Appendix to *Comedy*, *op cit.*, p. 252.

malign, and cast an oblique light on them, followed by valleys of silvery laughter. That is the Comic Spirit.[3]

Is this Meredith's subtle way of saying that God laughs? If so, he is sure that God's laughter comes only with an underlying interest in our welfare. The laughter is directed at our frailties, but its purpose is to heal. There are, of course, persons who are opposed to laughter, especially in religion, where they think of it as inappropriate or even sacrilegious. They would be shocked at the idea that there is any connection between God and the Comic Spirit. These are the people termed by Meredith "misogelastics," or laughter-haters. It is probable that, in coining this term, he had in mind the well-known passage in *The Phaedo*, in which Socrates tells his listeners what a terrible thing it is to become a misologist, or a hater of ideas.[4] The misologists and the misogelastics belong to the same intellectual family.

So important is humor in our effort to understand the mystery of existence that we have reason to doubt the excellence of a philosopher who does not exhibit, at some point, a humorous vein. Particularly should we doubt the philosopher who takes himself so seriously that he cannot laugh at his own pretensions. It is not sacrilegious to call humor the "jovial." To laugh is to see beyond the transitoriness of events, and thus to be Olympian or Jovelike.

Though Christ employed several types of humor, the most common type which He used is *irony*, i.e., a holding up to public view of either vice or folly, but without a note of bitterness or the attempt to harm. The ironical is always marked with a subtle sharpness of insight, free from the desire to wound. This is what distinguishes it most clearly from *sarcasm*. A number of examples can be assembled to illustrate this light

---

[3] *Comedy, op. cit.* p. 48.
[4] *Phaedo*, 89c ff. "No worse thing can happen to a man than this," said Socrates.

and delightful kind of humor. Whereas sarcasm tends to be cutting, irony may be playful. We are so familiar with irony of this character in Plato's dialogues that "Socratic irony" is a term deeply embedded in our language.

Socratic irony is feigned ignorance employed in such a way as to draw out and finally to confound an antagonist, though frequently the antagonist is not aware of what is happening to him. An important reason for our general familiarity with the humor of Socrates is his extraordinary good luck in his students, and particularly in Plato. "Socrates," says a great modern philosopher, "owes his immortality of fame as a martyr of philosophy not to any melodramatic outburst of popular sentiment on the part of an emotional democracy, but to the Providence which gave him as younger friend and follower the one man in history who has combined supreme greatness as a philosophic thinker with equal greatness as a master of language, and so has been, directly or indirectly, the teacher of all thinking men since his own day."[5]

The irony of Socrates is best expressed in his humility, either mock or real, in which the teacher becomes, at least for the moment, the taught, with Socrates exhibiting himself as eager to learn, even from those who are patently stupid. Socrates, at first, had high hopes of learning from those of a scientific turn of mind, but was progressively disappointed when they revealed their superficiality. This early disappointment led him, as he humorously put it, to conclude that he "had no head for the natural sciences." One consequence of this ironic self-deprecation was Socrates' decision to strike out on a line of investigation of his own, a decision which has influenced the entire subsequent course of human thought. The ironic humility of one who could not believe the word of the oracle about his alleged wisdom, and thus always sought to disprove the oracular

[5] A. E. Taylor, *Socrates* (New York: Doubleday & Company, 1956), p. 129.

judgment by finding greater wisdom in others, has been one of the most potent influences in all intellectual history.

When we realize that the use of irony is common to Socrates and to Christ we understand better why Edith Hamilton, whose death, even at a great age, has been such a blow to American letters, decided to include a chapter on Socrates in her Life of Christ.[6] We see Christ more truly, Miss Hamilton reasoned, if we see Socrates first, for most of us agree with Justin Martyr that the famous Athenian, who, like Christ, published nothing and whose execution was a victory, was a Christian before Christ.

Christ, so far as we know, did not resemble Socrates by leading people along until the position under examination exhibited its own illogicality or inner absurdity, but He did, sometimes, allow the logic of the situation to demonstrate itself by the use of the ironic question. The basic impact of the pragmatic teaching that any system is to be known primarily by its consequences is brought out by means of the question which requires no answer: "Are grapes gathered from thorns, or figs from thistles?" (Matt. 7:16). A similar approach is the answer to John's two emissaries, who asked him whether he was the Messiah. Christ did not answer their question directly, in the prosy manner the men sought, but gave the evidence and allowed them to answer themselves. "Go and tell John," He said, "what you have seen and heard: the blind receive their sight, the lame walk, lepers are cleansed, and the deaf hear, the dead are raised up, the poor have good news preached to them" (Luke 7:22). The allusion to Isaiah 61 was so patent, and would have been so clear to John, that it was not necessary to mention it.

Perhaps the most sly of all the bits of Gospel irony is the little touch about rewards. Jesus mentions the well-known practice of men who wish to advertise either their piety or their

[6] *Witness to the Truth, op. cit.*

benevolence, and rejects this as totally unworthy. "Beware," He says, "of practicing your piety before men in order to be seen by them" (Matt. 6:1). In regard to philanthropy He rejects, in our terms, the *bronze plaque*. "Thus, when you give alms, sound no trumpet before you, as the hypocrites do in the synagogues and in the streets, that they may be praised by men" (Matt. 6:2). All this is very clear, very straightforward, and not really funny. It is too sad to be funny, as we all know when we examine our own practice by this elevated standard. The sentence seems to bring the discussion to an end, *but it doesn't*, and therein lies the humorous twist. The punch is topped by the added line, "They have their reward." This says volumes and it is profoundly amusing.[7] Watch out what you want, He seems to say, for you are very likely to get it. Those interested in self-advertisement tend to be successful. The tragedy lies in their very success. Do you want status? It is not very hard to achieve.

The same ironic emphasis on the phrase "they have their reward" comes in connection with Christ's reference to those who suppose religion, to be genuine, has to be dull and sad (Matt. 6:16). It is in this context that Christ coins the pithy sentence used as the epigraph of Chapter I, "Do not look dismal." Some people, He says chaffingly, try to look dismal and they have their reward; *they succeed!*

One of the best examples of irony concerns John the Baptist, especially when Jesus is obviously teasing His hearers. We have already noted the passage in which Jesus pointed out the impossibility of pleasing the critics, since they didn't like His own feasting and also didn't like John's fasting. Just prior to this, Christ asked, teasingly, what it was that they expected (Luke 7:24-26). You object to his sternness and Puritanical teaching, do you? Well, what did you expect? Did you think you would see a Herod? Did you suppose you would

7 "All vulgar souls," said Renan, "are punished by their very vulgarity."

meet a man in the wilderness with fine clothing and living luxuriously? Such is a paraphrase of His question, a question which must have made His hearers realize the absurdity of their criticism. Of course, when He put it this way, they could see how ridiculous it was to object to John's violently couched method of speech. The teasing and ironical question was certain to be more effective than would have been a wholly serious and indicative approach.

Another illustration of light irony is that concerning preparation for the future. The serious teaching, of course, was a warning against anxiety and overconcern for the future, with a consequent neglect of the present. "Therefore I tell you, do not be anxious about your life, what you shall eat, nor about your body, what you shall put on" (Luke 12:22). With this we may associate the terse advice to take no thought for the morrow, for the morrow will take care of itself. The climactic line is to the effect that the evil of any particular day is wholly adequate, without borrowing any more: "Each day has troubles enough of its own" (Matt. 6:34, N.E.B.).

We are all familiar with the fact that some humorless and literal-minded Christians have used this teaching as an excuse to take out no insurance and even to have no savings. Of course, they are not able to be consistent or thorough in their literalistic application, since nobody can survive in the modern world without making engagements and participating in some forms of planning. A radical literalism would prohibit laying in food for the winter, as even the squirrels do. The birds may not have barns, but they do make nests for future use. They neither sow nor reap, but they go south for the winter. A foolish and self-defeating literalism, which may condemn a man's children to poverty in case of his early death, is one of the evil fruits of failing to see that Christ was joking. He is warning, by His sly exaggeration, against overdoing a good thing. If we are expecting humor, and therefore erect no psychological barrier to its reception, we are bound to smile, as a result of our own experience, when He says "Don't trouble about tomorrow. Tomorrow will be bad enough when it comes. Each day has enough trouble without bothering to borrow some extra." To miss this is to miss part of the abundance which Christ said He came to give.

One of the saddest of our failures to see Christ's humorous intent, and thus to sharpen our perception of the teaching, is found in our confusion about judgment. When, in a contemporary church, the members decide to try to practice reality of membership,[8] there are always some who profess to be shocked. Who are we, they ask with mock humility, to *exclude* anybody? They conveniently ignore Christ's own practice which, by erecting a costly standard, produced self-exclusion (Luke 9:57-62). They neglect the fact that He *warned*, and did not beg any one to enter the Cause, always pointing out that the price was high, the way narrow, and the recruits consequently few. We have already seen how violent was Christ's judgment of the Pharisees. He did not exclude them, but allowed them to exclude themselves. It is inconceivable that He would approve of accepting into membership those who are seeking chiefly social standing or respectability, and whose contribution in prayer or money or witness is intentionally nominal or trivial. Neglecting this entire side of Christ's message, the critics of a tough standard of entrance into membership fall back on the strategy of literalism and say that neither they nor anyone else can rightly make a judgment in such matters because Christ said, "Judge not" (Matt. 7:1 and Luke 6:37). The notion that there is subtle humor in Christ's dictum is seldom even examined. But let us see.

It is obvious that men must judge! If we give up judgment we give up almost everything which dignifies human life. We

[8] For an account of one bold effort to take membership seriously see Elizabeth O'Connor, *Call to Commitment*, (New York: Harper & Row, 1963).

are judging, and rightly so, between different men and different platforms, every time that we cast a vote. We judge colleges when we help our children to decide where to enroll. To say that one is as good as another would contribute to the complete undermining of the effort to achieve academic excellence. In art, if we do not judge between the authentic and the forged, the artistic effort is destroyed. And it is *men* who must do the judging, for there is nobody else available. To say that one church is as good as another would be to *harm* rather than to help the entire Christian movement. After all, some churches are financial rackets, with all assets vested in the name of the pastors. Some mean business and some do not. It is patently absurd to say that there should be no standard by which the qualifications for membership should be judged, because the acceptance of such a practice would mean the complete devaluation of membership. There is no cutting edge that is not narrow. Judgment may be mistaken and imperfect, but the only alternative to it, viz., the refusal to judge at all, is manifestly worse.

What then can Christ have meant? He is reported to have said, "Judge not, that you be not judged. For with the judgment you pronounce you will be judged" (Matt. 7:1, 2). Here the irony is particularly sharp. "You want to avoid judgment, do you?" He can be understood as saying, "Then be sure that you at least have the consistency to avoid it, yourself." It is of the essence of judgment that it is always two-edged. People will apply to you the standard which you apply to others, and so, indeed, they ought to do. "Do you criticize others for advertising their benevolences? Then you had better," says Christ, "examine your own practice, since an ethically honest man will never make an exception of himself. It is intrinsic to any moral order that every judgment is a self-judgment."

If this paraphrase is at all correct, we have here one of the most vivid examples of that kind of irony in which the intended implication is the exact opposite of the literal sense. What we have, in reality, is not the categorical command never to render judgment, a command which, if obeyed, would destroy all that is best in human life. What we have, instead, is the warning that if you want to avoid judgment on yourself, you will have to do the *impossible*, i.e., refuse to engage in any judgment at all. It is here that we find Christ's humor at its subtlest and deepest. It is not surprising that it sometimes escapes the insensitive.

If the ancients were like us they rejoiced in a big crowd. Both politicians and preachers have to be very sophisticated if they are to avoid the temptation to measure their effectiveness by the number of occupied seats. Accordingly, the big gatherings mentioned in the Gospels obviously impressed the disciples. And, of course, these *were* crowds. We read of five thousand men in the wilderness, and Matthew adds that this number did not include the women and children (Matt. 14:21). We also read that the people pressed on Jesus so that He was forced to get into a boat in order to speak to those on the shore (Mark 4:1). However much this may have impressed the disciples and the populace, we have a record of a humorous saying which shows that Christ, Himself, was not overimpressed. He said, possibly quoting a well-known aphorism, "Wherever the corpse is, there the vultures will gather" (Matt. 24:28, N.E.B.). In short, He recognized that there is more than one possible reason for the assembling of a crowd. It *may* mean something good, and it may not. As a matter of fact, His warning is given special significance when we realize that there is no evidence that a single one of the five thousand ever became a loyal follower. Perhaps some did, but, if so, we do not know it. In any case, Christ put His faith in the small Company and depended on them, rather than on the fickle crowds, for the perpetuation of His message.

That a gentle use of irony came early in Christ's public career is shown by His appeal to the very first of those who were willing to commit themselves to Him, and to His cause. These were two fishermen, Simon and Andrew, and He reached these first recruits by a witty reference to their occupation. It is hard to think that they did not smile when He said, "Follow me, and I will make you fishers of men" (Mark 1:17). The term "fishers of men" has, of course, become so much a part of our total language that it is not striking to us, but once it must have been. The irony is so slight that it could never produce a boisterous laugh, but it could elicit a smile.

Much more striking, as an example of Christ's irony, is the application of a nickname to one of these men, Simon (Matt. 16:18). Peter got his nickname when, in the district of Caesarea Philippi, he achieved, suddenly, the tremendous insight concerning who his Leader was. Even on this solemn occasion Christ proved that He could joke and He did so by giving Simon the fisherman the most improbable of nicknames. In our terminology, He called the fellow "Rocky" and the name stuck. The paradox is obvious, for Simon was anything but stable or durable, which is what rocky things are supposed to be. No sooner did Simon receive his nickname, Peter, than he rejected his Master's teaching and rebuked him, whereupon Christ said to him, with sudden fierceness, "Get behind me, Satan! You are a hindrance to me; for you are not on the side of God, but of men" (Matt. 16:23). That Peter was unstable was proved by his showing himself to be both a liar and a coward at the time of the trial before the high priest. Peter "followed at a distance" and sat in the courtyard, but when he was asked whether he was one of Christ's companions, he answered, "I do not know what you mean" (Matt. 26:71), and later said "I do not know the man."

If this was the "Rock" on which the redemptive fellowship had to be built, it certainly seemed to be a shaky foundation.

The house was obviously being built on sand, at best, and how, from such an infirm base, would it be possible to penetrate the very gates of hell? Here is paradox on paradox, yet it was more than a joke, though it *was* a joke. Jesus saw more in Simon and the other inadequate men than met the eye. The humorous nickname "Rocky" was a prediction of future stability, even though, at the time, it was patently absurd. At the moment, it must have seemed like our practice of calling the fat man "Slim" and the tall man "Shorty." But it was more than that. The very irony served a redemptive purpose, in that the power of expectancy was demonstrated in the revolutionary result. We do not know much about Peter's personal life, or about his wife, or even, apart from mere tradition, how he reached his end, but we do know that he preached the resurrection with persuasive power, that he recognized the necessity of liberation of all Christians from the bondage of the Hebrew law, and that he was a tower of strength in the infant church. The joke ceased to be merely a joke, because what began as shifting rubble was transformed, by the influence of the Living Christ, into solid rock. Peter he was not; but Peter he became! What started as joke ended as fact.

The dividing line which separates irony and sarcasm is sometimes a narrow one and is easily crossed. Truth compels us to say that it is sometimes crossed in the words recorded in the Gospels. In a few instances the irony becomes so exaggerated that it is really sarcastic. We do well to note carefully the instances of this, inasmuch as Christ must have felt that the gravity of some problems required a sterner treatment.

An excellent illustration is that about the keeping of the law. In Luke's account we read, "It is easier for heaven and earth to pass away, than for one dot of the law to become void" (Luke 16:17). The upholders of the law, committed to its very minutiae, were more concerned with it than with the whole of heaven and earth. The Pharisees could see the whole universe destroyed with more equanimity than they were able to muster if they witnessed hungry men rubbing out heads of wheat on the Sabbath or if they saw a man healed at a time when healing was ceremonially forbidden. Now the clear point is that Christ valued the world more than every jot and tittle of the law or even more than the entire law. We know this from the record of His own practice and from His emphasis upon mercy rather than upon sacrifice. If the Sabbath was made for man, rather than man for the Sabbath, then something in earth and heaven was more valuable than the law, including its most trivial details. The word "dot" is obviously meant to signify a trivial detail. These details were intimately connected with the ceremonial rules of the Temple, but Christ said boldly, "I tell you, something greater than the temple is here" (Matt. 12:6).

There is no evidence that the reporters of the pungent saying about its being easier to lose the world than to lose a detail of the law understood it as a joke at all. Very likely they missed the sarcasm, as some of us have done more recently. The seriousness with which the remark was received is indicated by the form which it is given in Matthew. "For truly, I say to you, till heaven and earth pass away, not an iota, not a dot, will pass from the law until all is accomplished." If this was sober truth, then we cannot avoid the conclusion that the early Christians who ceased to require circumcision and who rejected dietary laws were wholly wrong! If what Christ said was sober prose it was simply false! The only alternative solution is that He was joking. His words make sense only if they are exaggerated banter.

Why we miss so much of this, even today, requires some rational explanation. Why, for instance, do we miss the sarcasm about courts of law which appears in both Matthew and Luke? Whatever else we can say about Christ's teaching,

the main tenor of it was not that of prudence or of compromise. Indeed, we are told that the deepest things are
hidden from the wise and prudent, i.e., the people who know
how to look out for number one (Matt. 11:25). But what
are we to make of this counsel of prudence?

As you go with your accuser before the magistrate, make an
effort to settle with him on the way, lest he drag you to the judge,
and the judge hand you over to the officer, and the officer put
you in prison. I tell you, you will never get out till you have paid
the very last copper. [Luke 12:58, 59]

Because we are familiar with these words, we fail to see how
shocking they are. Because we are so bemused by the desire
to make them creditable, we twist them into a preconceived
pattern. But what do the words really say? Here is a picture
of the clear miscarriage of justice which must have been all
too familiar to Christ's original hearers. The rude fishermen
might miss some of the finer points of irony, but they could
hardly miss the sarcasm about justice. They knew what it was
to have the last copper exacted, even though the offense was
minor or even though the charge was unjust.

What Christ seems to be advocating is a clever deal or a
bribe. Pay off your accuser or fix it up with him somehow,
regardless of justice! Translated into our language, "It may
prove to be cheaper to pay the officer than to pay the court, so
why not try?" Perhaps that would be the path of wisdom
in a world where leading men "bind heavy burdens, hard to
bear, and lay them on men's shoulders; but they themselves
will not move them with their finger" (Matt. 23:4). If this be
humor, it is humor with an acid touch. The account of
going before the judges is so vivid that it sounds like the
voice of experience. It is not unreasonable to suppose that
Christ had already been in their clutches. But that the
prudential advice is sarcastic is indicated by the fact that it

is preceded immediately by a vivid query completely at variance with the acceptance of mere prudential advice: "And why do you not judge for yourselves what is right?" (Luke 12:57). Here is the antithesis of supine accommodation to unjust treatment. And then the point is driven home, for those willing and able to see it, by a lampoon.

CHAPTER IV

◆§؛◆

The Strategy of Laughter

> O Lord, make my enemies ridiculous.
> *Voltaire*

CHRIST HAD TO WAGE a battle because the things for which He stood were intrinsically threatening to those in power, either politically or religiously. The fierceness of the struggle made choice necessary and with choice came inevitable division among men. The people who wanted to smooth things over and to be friends with everybody, thus avoiding all tension, were simply naïve, for life is not ordered that way. Herein lies the tremendous import of Christ's words, "Do not think that I have come to bring peace on earth; I have not come to bring peace, but a sword" (Matt. 10:34). Luke amplifies the saying by adding, "No, I tell you, but rather division" (Luke 12:51), and both Matthew and Luke elaborate the point by showing how Christ's mission will even bring trouble in families. Is Christ referring to the apparent failure of His own mother and brothers to appreciate His work when, according to Matthew, He adds, "and a man's foes will be those of his own household" (Matt. 10:36)?

The way in which the sharp message about the rejection of all easy peace is couched makes it likely that Christ was already finding it necessary to counteract a false reputation. By prefacing His statement, "Do not think," He indicated that some *did* think. Negative commandments never refer to what no one is tempted to do. This is why it is said, with both cynicism and truth, that a sound sociological device for discovering the actual behavior of a people is to learn what their prohibitions are. It is reasonable to conclude that the picture of "Gentle Jesus, meek and mild" had already, in His earthly lifetime, begun to be fastened upon Him. Therefore He had to do something to blast the picture. The mere fact that it was at variance with experience had not proved adequate for its destruction.

Christ's continual battle for the minds of those about Him required the use of a wide variety of weapons. In His arsenal were expressions of proverbial wisdom, which people would recognize and respect, as well as new epigrams and parables based upon the common life of the common people. It is not known to us, and it is not important that it be known, how many of these expressions were wholly or partly proverbial. It was not necessary for His purpose that all that He said should be original. That it was *not* all original is shown by the well-known quotations from the Hebrew Scriptures and His adaptation of the words of John. Perhaps part of His humor arose from His love of Psalm 100, with its striking line, "Serve the Lord with gladness" (A.V.).

Whether His epigrams were original or not is immaterial, because, in the latter case, He was demonstrating His ability to take the commonplace and to give it added currency, while, in the former, His original sayings were *becoming* maxims. "A maxim is," as Coleridge said, "a conclusion upon observation of matters of fact."[1] The clearest example of Christ's use of a maxim, in the strategy of intellectual battle, is that to the effect that a prophet is honored in all countries except his own (Mark 6:4, Matt. 13:57, Luke 4:24). This, which

[1] *Writings on Shakespeare, op cit.,* p. 167.

represents the distillation of wisdom from observed experience, may be very old indeed, and may be a quotation. We are reminded of the way in which, when Aristophanes introduces[2] the aphorism, "We can't live with women, but we can't live without them," he represents the witty remark as a quotation from a humorous predecessor. Augustine, likewise, refuses to take the credit for one of his best jokes. Genius lies in keeping a maxim from becoming a platitude. It is almost certain to undergo this fate unless there is a humorous twist.

The maxim about lack of honor in a prophet's own country is associated, in Luke's account, with what Christ acknowledges to be a proverb, "Doubtless you will quote to me this proverb, 'Physician, heal yourself'" (Luke 4:23), but Luke does not include, as Matthew does, the reference to one's own house or, what is even more significant, to one's own kin, which Mark preserves. Is there bitter irony in the elaboration of the supposed proverb to include a sly reference to Christ's own home and family?

Some readers may remember a vivid section of Nathaniel Micklem's book, *The Galilean*, termed "On Being Misunderstood at Home."[3] When Mariolatry is a real danger in contemporary Christendom, Professor Micklem's reminder is highly relevant. Whatever the later tradition about Christ's mother may have become, "the New Testament itself seems almost to go out of its way to explain that, for all her prayers and expectations, she did not really understand her son; his mother as well as his brothers did not 'believe on him'; and we must realize that part of the Cross which Jesus had to bear was that he, like his disciples, had to forsake mother and home and had, as he said, to 'hate' father and mother, yes. and 'his own soul also,' for the sake of the Gospel. If only his mother had stood by him through those lonely years; if only

[2] In *Lysistrata*.
[3] London: James Clarke and Company, 1923, pp. 29-31.

she had been what tradition would make out! We can imagine the heart-sickness which were his when he said that whoever does God's will is his mother and sister and brother."[4] We have been strangely oblivious to Christ's devastating rejoinder to the woman in the crowd who said, with mere sentimentality, "Blessed is the womb that bore you, and the breasts that you sucked!" (Luke 11:27). Jesus brushed this aside with terrible brevity, saying, "Blessed rather are those who hear the word of God and keep it!"

Micklem goes on, as we would expect, to point out that, though at the beginning Mary sought to restrain Christ (Mark 3:31), at the end she came up to Jerusalem amongst His followers, that she was with Him at the last, and that she was in the company of those who believed on Him after the resurrection. But all this was long after He had adapted the presumed proverb to His own condition. In spite of the sadness, such adaptation is on the verge of humor.

The brief and originally misunderstood metaphor of the two leavens, that of the Pharisees on one side and that of Herod on the other, gives an important clue to Christ's struggle. He saw, at the start, that the fundamental dangers were not single, but were dual or even multiple. It is always true, so far as can be seen, that any possible alternative to a particular error *may* be another error. If the only alternative to an error were the truth, life would be simple, but that is precisely what life never is. Therefore, since the possibilities of evil are plural, we must beware of moving from one of these to another. There is no advantage in escaping from the fire into the frying pan. Similarly, there would be no gain, the metaphor suggests, in avoiding the dominance of Herod, only to fall into the clutches of the Pharisees or vice versa. There is not much to choose between the dictatorship of the Right and the dictatorship of the Left.

[4] *Ibid.*, pp. 30-31.

HEROD

Like almost all who valued the Hebrew heritage, Christ apprehended the threat represented by the Herodian dynasty. When Herod the Great, a tool of the Roman power, died in 4 B.C., it was the desire of the religious community of Jerusalem that the Herodian rule, which they naturally hated, should be dissolved. But the Roman authorities decided that its continuation was politically useful. They followed the dead father's expressed wishes by dividing the territory among his three sons, the northeast going to Philip, Galilee and Transjordan going to Herod Antipas, and Samaria and Judea going to Archelaus. Archelaus was deposed in A.D. 6 and his territory put under a Roman procurator who resided in Caesarea and was military commander-in-chief of the area. It was Herod Antipas, the puppet ruler of Galilee, who beheaded John the Baptist and later became worried about the public influence of Jesus.[5]

Christ hated all that Herod Antipas stood for in his rule of orgiastic splendor and self-indulgence. The account of Herod's imprisonment of John, as the result of a woman's intrigue, and John's foul murder, receives its fullest and most vivid expression in Mark 6:17-29, though a shorter version occurs in Matthew 14:3-12 and a very short one in Luke 3:19-20. Herod, the tetrarch, when he heard of the work of Jesus, sought to see him (Luke 9:9) because there was a rumor that Jesus was really John raised from the dead, and the superstitious man wanted to see for himself. But when Pilate finally sent Jesus to Herod in Jerusalem, the tetrarch received little satisfaction, for he was not able to get a word out of Christ (Luke 23:8, 9). Herod, we are told, treated Christ with contempt,

---

[5] We are fortunate in having from Abingdon Press two illuminating and scholarly volumes regarding the Herods. They are *The life and times of Herod the Great* and *The Later Herods*, both by Stuart H. Perowne, and published in America in 1958.

and mocked Him by decking Him out in gorgeous apparel, presumably because of the charge about Kingship, which was something that involved a potential threat to his own status.

Dangerous as men of the character of Herod and Pilate were, Christ was able to maintain some sense of humor in regard to them. This is shown by Christ saying of Herod, "Go and tell that fox" (Luke 13:32). The humorous point can be appreciated without emphasizing, as is sometimes done, the fact that the Greek word for fox is feminine in gender. Jesus, presumably, did not speak Greek, but fox means the same in any language. He could tease, even about a man as dangerous as the one who had murdered His friend.

Christ's strategy, on the days preceding the crucifixion, is revealing. Not only did He frustrate Herod's desire by His absolute silence; to Pilate He gave what must have been the most frustrating of answers, the laconic "You said it." All of the Synoptics agree that when Pilate asked "Are you the King of the Jews?" Christ's only reply was "You have said so." The result of this strategy was that "Pilate wondered" (Mark 15:5). We realize, as we read the Gospels, that we cannot expect humor in the tragic chapters in the degree to which we find it earlier, but even here, in the laconic "The words are yours," we find the closest approximation to humor that is compatible with such deep tragedy. The Roman commander had unlimited power to enable him to order the execution of this Disturber, but he had no absolute insurance against the strategy which made him temporarily ridiculous. We are reminded of the words of the Emperor Julian, "Thou hast conquered, O Galilean."

THE PHARISEES

Though the battle of Christ had to be waged on two fronts, one of these occupied far more time and effort than did the other. This was the front against the religious opposition, represented primarily by the enmity of the Pharisees. Here the strategy of laughter was more appropriate and effective than on the political front, for bigotry is peculiarly vulnerable to ridicule. It is surprising to some, though it ought not to be, that Christ's most intractable enemies were those who saw, in Him and His teaching, a threat to their own religious program. While the Roman power, vested in the procurator, must be held accountable for His actual execution, the truth is that the procurator acted reluctantly, and that the development would not have moved to its tragic end had it not been for the fierce enmity engendered in the members of the Sanhedrin. Religious enemies are the fiercest that there are! Because we really know this, we give full assent to Pascal's famous epigram, "Men never do evil so completely and cheerfully as when they do it from religious conviction."

Christ's major weapon against the Pharisaic attack was laughter, and He used it fully. The point at which they were most vulnerable was their manifest self-righteousness. There is no doubt that, in one way, the Pharisees were good men. They saw the evils of laxity and the best of them made a great effort to be consistent in practicing the law. They agreed with Jesus that the way is narrow, and they sincerely tried to follow it. They were, quite consciously, "the Pious" (Chassidim) and they accepted, without compromise, the effort to keep rigorously to the commands of the Torah in all phases of common life. They are not to be confused with the priestly caste which was often somewhat secularized.

The beginning reader of the Gospels is often surprised to find how much more critical attention Jesus gives to the Pharisees than to the priests. The clear reason is that the Pharisees were actually and potentially far the more powerful, because they were much closer to the common man. They exhibited an undoubted dedication, which is always a source of power, though it is not always a power for good. After all, the characteristic follower of the Communist party line, whether Chinese or Russian, is normally a deeply and fiercely dedicated man. Professor Bornkamm has been helpful in his clear presentation of the virtues and the attendant dangers of the Pharisaism which Christ found that He had to oppose.

The Pharisees are a lay movement, joined closely together in a community of their own. The Pharisees quite definitely are innovators; not, as is often erroneously thought, a conservative reactionary group. For their zeal is aimed at this: the law is not to be left merely in its sacrosanct letter, but it is to be interpreted as obligatory for the present day, and to be applied to all problems of private and public life.[6]

Now it should be clear that such people were not to be taken lightly. Since these men were not priests, they could not be dismissed as being professionally religious. Furthermore, they tried to make religion relevant to the contemporary life of Palestine. Their worship was not directed to the Temple, where priests officiated, but rather to the synagogue, a far more significant religious institution in the long run, partly because its units could be so numerous. The Christian Church, when it developed, was by no means identical with the synagogue, but was, nevertheless, far closer to it than to the Temple, with its concentration upon priestly sacrifices and ritual. The invention of the synagogue, during or after the exile, as a conscious effort to solve the religious problem of the refugees who were unable any longer to use the Temple, is one of the most revolutionary in religious history.[7] The synagogue or meetinghouse was not a Temple at all, but was an institution limited deliberately to instruction in the law, to the reading and ex-

[6] Gunther Bornkamm, *Jesus of Nazareth* (New York: Harper & Row, 1960), pp. 39, 40.
[7] See George Foot Moore, *Judaism in the First Centuries of the Christian Era*, Vol. I, pp. 281 ff. It was often said by Jewish scholars, during his great days of teaching at Harvard, that Moore understood Judaism better than they did.

position of the Hebrew Scriptures, to confession and prayer. Whoever started this institution, about a half millennium before Christ, was a genuine innovator, for it is something "for which there is no parallel in the ancient history of religion."[8]

It is important that we appreciate the great value of the synagogue which was, for years, the only means of holding a dispersed Judaism together. The old system was inoperable, since many Jews were too far from Jerusalem to go there and since the Temple building was, for a time, destroyed anyway. When we appreciate its value we see why the Pharisees were so closely associated with the scribes. The very loyalty to the text of Scripture led, paradoxically, to scribal additions or expositions, since the Scripture required explanation. These explanations tended to achieve an authoritative status of their own. The obligatory expositions sometimes involved the most subtle casuistry, and this became an obvious target for Christ's ironical thrusts.

The Pharisees were, in a sense, Reformers and they displayed the fanatical zeal of any true Reformation. Again, Bornkamm is helpful at this point:

> The entire life of the individual from morning till night was ritualized to the minutest detail, with prayer and cleansing regulations, with rules for eating and for relations with other people. Above all, the observance of the Sabbath rest became an inexhaustible topic, as we know from Jesus' numerous conflicts and disputes, and also from the literature of the rabbis. Is it permissible on the Sabbath to rescue an animal which has fallen into the well? To eat an egg laid on the Sabbath day? To keep food hot on the fire? May one get engaged?[9]

If Pharisaism had been all bad it would not have justified so sustained and varied an attack. The fact that many of the Pharisees exhibited a rigorous desire to attain moral purity

[8] Bornkamm, *op. cit.*, p. 40.
[9] *Ibid.*, p. 40.

helps us to see why Christ gave them so much more attention than He gave to the Sadducees, who belonged chiefly to the privileged priestly families of Jerusalem. Lacking the intensity of the Pharisees, the Sadducees could, far more easily, make concessions to the secular power and to the surrounding paganism. As far as the actual priests in the Temple area were concerned, Jesus could afford to ignore them almost completely, for they exhibited nothing comparable to the zeal of the dedicated lay group.

Jesus had to attack the Pharisees much as Socrates had to attack the Sophists, because in both cases the public was bound to make a facile identification. Socrates and the Sophists were both concerned with human problems, while Jesus and the Pharisees were both calling for commitment. Because He must have appeared, superficially, to be like the Pharisees, Christ had to be unusually careful to make the sharp distinction. The disciples of Jesus and the disciples of the Pharisees (Mark 2:18) were both committed groups, but the object of commitment was not the same, and that made all the difference.

It was the great merit of the Pharisees that they tried to take their religion seriously. They sought to make, not a mere gesture, but a real effort to attain righteousness. In short, they were perfectionists, never permitting themselves the laxity of frequent exceptions to the rule. They were not, therefore, like those who say that they will start tomorrow. Their great mistake, however, was the supposition that, because they adhered so rigorously to the rule of perfection, they had actually attained it. They were bound to be caught in the trap of all self-righteousness, viz., that they could perform all the externals of the code, but could not thereby become fully righteous internally. This, of course, is Christ's point about the contrast between the inside and the outside of the cup.

The moral teaching of Christ, in sharp contrast to that of the

Pharisees, was centered upon the conviction that all of the major sins, like all of the major virtues, are inner ones. Since these are matters of the heart, they cannot be observed directly by others, yet from them flow all of the important events of life. This teaching was emphasized by the special preface used for great occasions: "Hear me, all of you, and understand: there is nothing outside a man which by going into him can defile him; but the things which come out of a man are what defile him" (Mark 7:14, 15). It is because of this central moral fact that no man is wholly pure. Absolute purity would involve motives as well as deeds, but what man can say sincerely that his motives will bear full examination? The spectacular penetration of Dostoyevsky's moral analysis in *The Brothers Karamazov* receives most of its merit from the author's evident dependence on the teaching of Jesus at this point. Which son killed the father? Was the crime, and consequent punishment, limited to the one who performed the material deed? What about the others who also desired his death? Dostoyevsky makes this inquiry so vivid that even the sensitive reader feels like a murderer.

In no area of experience was the righteousness of men such as the Pharisees more vulnerable than in that of sex. There is, of course, no reason to doubt that the stern moralists maintained, successfully, a high standard of external behavior in this regard. They avoided fornication and adultery and they were not softly permissive regarding the conduct of others who sinned in this way. Apparently they supposed that this was the end of the matter, but, in supposing so, they did not reckon with the half-humorous probing provided by the Nazarene. Christ's method of attack was to expand the scope of adultery to include all of its inner springs of imagination and desire. "You have learned," He said, "that they were told, 'Do not commit adultery.' But what I tell you is this: If a man looks on a woman with a lustful eye, he has already committed adultery with her in his heart" (Matt. 5:27-28, N.E.B.).

By such an analysis the self-righteousness of the critics of Jesus, or of anybody else, is completely undermined. What ordinary healthy man can honestly claim that he has not looked on a great many attractive women with desire in his heart? There is, as everyone knows, the lust of the eye, and it is far removed from perfect purity. There is no man more vulnerable and therefore more ridiculous than the one who claims to be perfect. Human perfection is a worthwhile goal, providing we are realistic enough to know that we do not attain it. But the man who claims attainment is wide open to attack. This was the Achilles' heel of the Pharisaic party and Christ did not hesitate to strike it. By making all men, including His critics, adulterers, He laughed away righteous pretense. The strategy of laughter is directed toward all who suppose that, by rules, they can solve the problem of sin. It is too deep for that.

Man is a creature who has an unending desire to be logical, in the sense of being consistent, yet he is well aware of the fact that all of his life is riddled with inconsistency. Because we are aware of inconsistency in ourselves, we are potentially aware of inconsistencies everywhere, and, when they are not too painful, as in the development of actual mental illness, we laugh. Herein lies the permanent humorous appeal of the well-known joke known as "the robber robbed." Every wiseacre who falls into his own trap illustrates this. It is the same as the seducer seduced, and is illustrated in the Gospel when the self-righteous and puritanical are shown to be adulterers. The only known examples of true humor in the Fourth Gospel turn on this theme. The first is that of the woman at the well of Samaria who asked pious questions, but, according to Jesus, did not tell the whole truth (John 4:18). The second is the passage of doubtful authenticity about the woman taken in adultery, and the humor lies in Christ's revelation of the inconsistency of the critics. The ridiculous contradiction is apparent when Christ says that the one who is totally innocent may cast the first stone.[10]

We have often missed the element of banter in Christ's handling of the woman at the well of Samaria. If He eventually saw through the sexual irregularity of this woman's life, He must have seen it at the beginning. Why then did He say, "Go home, call your husband and come back" (N.E.B.)? The only reasonable explanation is that He was teasing and used this method to get her to tell the truth. Any assumption contrary to known fact is amusing, and in this case it was a useful weapon. The New English Bible brings out the humorous flavor of the episode when it makes Christ say, "You are right in saying that you have no husband, for, although you have had five husbands, the man with whom you are now living is not your husband; you told me the truth there." The sly insinuation is that she was not universally meticulous about the truth.

At another level of attack Christ examined the consistency of those who claimed to keep the entire law. Such a claim involves self-delusion and many subtle evasions, though the Pharisees did not seem to recognize their own circumventions. They began the controversy by criticizing the practice of Christ's followers of eating without previous ceremonial washing of hands. "And the Pharisees and the scribes asked him, 'Why do your disciples not live according to the tradition of the elders?'" (Mark 7:5). Christ's answer was to appeal first to the words of Isaiah, whom His opponents honored, by quoting the words, "This people honors me with their lips, but

[10] While the story of the woman taken in adultery has no fixed place in the ancient manuscripts of the Fourth Gospel and, therefore, is not printed in the regular text of the Revised Standard Version, as it is in the Authorized Version, it is not to be neglected. J. B. Phillips is making this clear when he says, "Almost all scholars would agree that, although the story is out of place here (John 7:53-8:11), it is part of a genuine apostolic tradition." *The New Testament in Modern English* (London: Geoffrey Bles, 1960), p. 550.

their heart is far from me; in vain do they worship me, teaching as doctrines the precepts of men" (Isa. 29:13 and Mark 7:6, 7). The requirement is to distinguish between the divine commandment and the accumulation of human tradition.

The first step in this rejoinder was hard to answer, but the second was more difficult still. He accused them of manipulating the rules, when it suited their purpose to do so. Here is one of the few instances similar to those mentioned at the end of Chapter III, in which Christ used what can only be called sarcasm. This is obvious when Mark reports Him as prefacing His statement about evasions by saying, "You have a fine way of rejecting the commandment of God" (Mark 7:9). All translations bring out the mock admiration. Christ spoke as though the ability to put on a legalistic act was something worthy of praise, but this had to be humorous, for He certainly did not admire what they were doing.

The point of the teaching is that the high claim to legal perfection is spoiled by the practice of conventionalized dodges. There were many possible illustrations available to Him, but the one He chose to emphasize was that regarding the fifth of the Ten Commandments, the commandment to honor one's parents. This, of course, if it is taken seriously and is not merely ceremonial, will involve provision of support for parents when they need it. But there was a tricky way around this and Jesus was aware of it. "But you say, 'If a man tells his father or his mother, What you would have gained from me is Corban' (that is, given to God) then you no longer permit him to do anything for his father or mother, thus making void the word of God through your tradition which you hand on" (Mark 7:11-13).[11]

Since it is not hard to see that this method of evasion can

[11] Bultmann exclaims, "How easy it is to nullify the fifth commandment by claiming priority for the ceremonial law." Rudolf Bultmann, *Primitive Christianity in Its Contemporary Setting* (New York: Meridian Books, 1957), p. 74.

be expanded endlessly, Jesus attacks it by making it laughable. Of course, by such tricks any rule can be bypassed. In our own day there are men who will tell you, humorlessly, that they are giving full obedience to the Old Testament law which prohibits shaving the beard, when they look as clean shaven as other men. The device, they say, is to use an electric razor and then no blade actually touches the skin of the face. What is really amazing is the ability of men to engage in such nullification without laughing at themselves. They could not do it with Jesus around. He was not opposed to keeping the commandments; what he opposed was pious cheating.

Nothing was more clear, in the movement which Christ began, than the practice of healing. This was not limited to Christ's own efforts, but was central to the work of the hard core of men on whom He depended, and to whose training he gave such careful attention. In commissioning this Gideon's band, the work which we call psychological healing was primary. "And he called the twelve together and gave them power and authority over all demons and to cure diseases, and he sent them out to preach the kingdom of God and to heal" (Luke 9:1, 2). This aspect of the work could not escape attention which included even a grudging admiration. People who were mentally ill became well and were able to live normal lives. Here was an objective demonstration which was far more effective than endless speculations and disputations. It was by reference to such evidence, rather than by words, that Jesus answered the emissaries of John. "In that hour he cured many of diseases and plagues and evil spirits" (Luke 7:21).

That the Apostles were meant to share in the ministry of healing is beyond doubt. When, after the disappointing experience at the synagogue of Nazareth, Christ exposed His new strategy of penetration of common life, "he called to him the twelve, and began to send them out two by two, and gave them authority over the unclean spirits" (Mark 6:7). Since

Christ's enemies could not claim, with any credibility, that healing did not occur, their only recourse was to try to find fault with the way in which it was done. On the principle that it requires a thief to catch a thief, they said that His very success, in expelling demons, meant that He was Himself demon-possessed, and in an extreme fashion. "And the scribes who came down from Jerusalem said, 'He is possessed by Beelzebul, and by the prince of demons he casts out the demons'" (Mark 3:22).

Obviously Christ had to answer this charge, which might easily impress the ignorant, but how was He to do it? Again we find Him using the strategy of laughter. "And if I cast out demons by Beelzebul, by whom do your sons cast them out?" (Matt. 12:27). The laugh is turned on the critics, since everyone who listens will realize that the subtle question has no possible answer. Either they do *not* cast them out, in which case they look silly, or, as is more likely, if they claim to be effective in this effort, they have already, by implication, suggested that they also are possessed. Christ's question really means, "By what demonic agency do you perform your miracles?"[12] It is easy to see that the humorous question is a far more effective rejoinder than would have been a serious argument about demons. The severest critics of Christ could not stand ridicule, for seriousness was their central strength.

It is in the collection of attacks reported in the twenty-third chapter of Matthew that we find the essence of Christ's strategy of laughter against the scribes and Pharisees. The vigorous attack begins with mock respect, which has a sharp barb in it. "The scribes and the Pharisees sit on Moses' seat; so practice and observe whatever they tell you, but not what they do" (Matt. 23:2, 3). The contrast between preaching and practice was inherently humorous, especially when it appeared

---

[12] I owe to Professor Alexander Purdy the idea that Christ's critics may actually have claimed to cast out demons themselves.

in men of such high pretensions. In this collection of criticisms provided by Matthew there are several which we have already mentioned, such as the cleansing of the outside of the cup and straining at a gnat while swallowing a camel. In similar vein He accused them, half-humorously, of assuming the posture of the dog in the manger. "But woe to you, scribes and Pharisees, hypocrites! because you shut the kingdom of heaven against men; for you neither enter yourselves, nor allow those who would enter to go in" (Matt. 23:13).

In regard to the prophets, Jesus employs the same essential joke which Bernard Shaw employed in his play *St. Joan*. It is conventional to admire the prophets after the lapse of years, but we might find them exceedingly disturbing if they were to be alive now. When Joan proposes to use her great power and come back to life, the proposal is naturally rejected with some panic. The only bearable prophets are dead ones! "Woe to you, scribes and Pharisees, hypocrites! for you build the tombs of the prophets and adorn the monuments of the righteous, saying 'If we had lived in the days of our fathers, we would not have taken part with them in shedding the blood of the prophets'" (Matt. 23:29, 30). Nearly all who read Plato's *Apology* assume, as a matter of course, that, if they had lived in Athens in 399 B.C., and had been among the judges of Socrates, they would have lined up with the minority who voted in his favor. But a little more sense of humor makes us wonder.

Few features of official religion, of any particular faith, are more open to ridicule than is ostentation. The Christian faith, which began with an emphasis upon simplicity and humility, as vividly illustrated by the acted parable of the washing of the disciples' feet, has succumbed, in various generations, to the temptation to grandeur. Christ saw it coming and gave advance warning, though the warning has been seldom heeded. He warned against such ceremonial titles as "Rabbi," i.e.

"Doctor" and "Father" and "Master" (Matt. 23:8-10) and He prefaced this by showing how ridiculous the scribes made themselves by their little works of pride which distinguished them from other men.[13] Did no one laugh when He said of them, "they make their phylacteries broad and their fringes long" (Matt. 23:5)? He went on to say that they reveled in being invited to sit at the head table at feasts (Matt. 23:6). Mark's version of this humorous exposure is, "Beware of the scribes, who like to go about in long robes, and to have salutations in the market places and the best seats in the synagogues and the places of honor at feasts" (Mark 12:38, 39). It is not really surprising that this text comes to the mind of a good many literate men while attending college commencements or church suppers. Presumption is not confined to synagogues.

THE PRIESTS

Though Christ's strategy of laughter was directed more to the Pharisaic party than to any other of the religious groups, it was not limited to them. The priests, though mentioned relatively little, came in for their share, too. The best instance of this is found in the captious question, asked by the priests and elders, and reported by all three Synoptics, demanding to know the ground of Christ's authority. What this meant was that they were assuming the necessity of an ecclesiastic system, the upholders of which are always worried by novelty. The Jerusalem elders were disturbed in much the manner of the English bishops of the eighteenth century, who were puzzled by the irregularity of John Wesley in contenancing a new episcopal system in the Methodist Church of America.

---

[13] The self-application of such titles is laughable because they are intrinsically pompous. Note Robert Frost's use of this in "A Hundred Collars" where he has a teacher introduce himself to his hotel roommate as Doctor Magoon.

Of course, Christ refused to be drawn into a direct answer to the question about authority, for that would have meant the tacit assumption of their basic premise, the supposition that, in religious matters, some chain of human authority is required. So he used the device of another question and asked them about the authority of John. This placed the priests and elders in a dilemma for, if they said that John's authority was divine, they would not have any valid objection to him, and, by extension, no valid objection to Christ, whereas, if they said it was merely human, i.e., of John's own private initiative, they would antagonize the people who had greatly admired the prophet of the wilderness. The strategy is succinctly phrased by Hussey when he says of Christ, "He does not make the mistake of floundering after an impossible reply; his weapon is counter-query, banteringly phrased, still more unanswerable."[14]

The strategy of counter-query was used, as well as known, on more than one occasion. It was used with marked effectiveness in the encounter with the combined forces of the Pharisees and the Herodians, their common hatred of Christ making them temporary allies. To their artful question about whether Roman taxes were lawful, he refused the kind of direct Yes or No which they sought, when they hoped to place Him in an awkward position with either answer. By asking of them the question about the likeness of the Emperor on the coin, Christ opened the way to His statement of the enduring principle of a rational division of responsibilites, so heralded by Lord Acton and others in their accounts of the development of political theory.[15] His opponents marveled as they departed (Matt. 22:22) and Luke says that they were silent (Luke

---

[14] L. M. Hussey, "The Wit of the Carpenter," in *The American Mercury*, Vol. V, p. 332.

[15] "These words gave to the civil power, under the protection of conscience, a sacredness it had never enjoyed and bounds it had never acknowledged; and they were also the repudiation of absolutism and the inauguration of freedom." *The History of Freedom in Antiquity.*

20:26), but was there also a sly smile? It would not have been surprising if there were. In any case we know that when the attack of the Sadducees also failed, "they no longer dared to ask him any question" (Luke 20:40).

The Disciples

Even the disciples, though they were not adversaries, came in for their share of banter. What else can we call it when Jesus, having already given Simon one nickname, momentarily gives him another by calling him "Satan"? (Matt. 16:23). Perhaps the most serious of all the failures of the Apostles to understand their Master was that which began with the argument about their precedence and status. Both Matthew and Mark place this argument during the final journey to Jerusalem, but Luke, with terrible paradox, places it in the midst of the Last Supper. Perhaps the problem arose more than once, since it is a problem inherent in the human situation. In Mark's account, James and John are represented as those who started the inquiry into status, with specific reference to their own. In Matthew's version, however, their ambitious mother does it for them, while in Luke's account the personalities are removed altogether. But in each case it is the same problem of complete failure to understand the revolutionary nature of Christ's teaching. They cannot see that He is proposing an order in which the question of status is rendered irrelevant. This is the reason why the symbolic foot washing was necessary.

We are grateful to Luke for preserving the only touch of humor in this important incident, for we can well believe that, in a problem of this character, laughter was the best weapon. The touch of humor that remains is found in the word "Benefactors." The translation of the New English Bible brings the point out vividly: "Then a jealous dispute broke out: who among them should rank highest? But he said, 'In the world, kings lord it over their subjects; and those in authority are called their country's "Benefactors." Not so with you: on the contrary, the highest among you must bear himself like the youngest, the chief of you like a servant. For who is greater —the one who sits at table or the servant who waits on him? Surely the one who sits at table. Yet here am I among you like a servant'" (Luke 22:24-27).

We cannot doubt that this highly revolutionary doctrine, which has not yet been taken seriously, even in the church, was made more understandable by the satire on the sort of name which a dictator likes to assume. It need not be "Benefactor," for it can also be "Liberator" or "Protector," or many more. Of course, the man who is in love with power, and who is clever enough to make the people idolize him, must always try to appear as one who has nothing but the people's interest at heart, but Christ knew better and, by His humor, may have been able to make the dull Apostles see a little way into the realm of pretense which is always involved in the love of prestige and power. This situation cannot be wholly changed, and it has not been materially changed to our day, but the strategy of laughter is still the most effective approach. One of the many valuable contributions to our understanding of Christ was made by T. R. Glover at this point. He showed how Christ could, at one stroke, infuse an old theme with both novelty and sly humor. "Did none of his disciples," Glover asked, "mark a touch of irony when he said that among the Gentile dynasties the kings who exercise authority are called 'Benefactors'? It was true; Euergetes is a well-known kingly title, but the explanation that it was the reward for strenuous use of monarchic authority was new. Are we to think his face gave no sign of what he was doing? Was there no smile?"[16]

[16] *The Jesus of History, op. cit.,* p. 49.

Both Donald Hankey and T. R. Glover saw Christ's use of the strategy of laughter at about the same time. Just before he entered the trenches of the First World War Hankey wrote:

The courage and good deeds of Jesus, His freedom from conventionality and puritanism, His hard rough life, His direct simplicity and unswerving faith, His crisp incisive judgments, and the keen satire with which He crumpled up the sophistries of the legal mind—all these things appealed to sinners and plain folk, who were sick to death of the eternal wranglings of their religious leaders about tradition and precedent. And they were responsible for the inclusion in the circle of disciples of many men of a type which never before and never since have felt themselves welcome in religious societies.[17]

[17] Donald Hankey, *The Lord of all Good Life* (London: Longmans, Green and Company, 1918), pp. 64, 65.

CHAPTER V

❧❧

Humorous Parables

The advantage of the parable is that
it is easily remembered.

Donald Hankey

A<small>CCORDING</small> TO the Synoptic Gospels the parable was
Christ's chief way of presenting His teaching. In this regard,
as in many others, there is a sharp and easily observable contrast between the Synoptics and the Fourth Gospel. There are
no parables in John, though there may be remnants of parables which appear in the form of allegories. Instead of parables
about shepherds we find "I am the good shepherd" (John
10:11) and general statements about shepherding, but no
story. In John's account, this is called a "figure" (John 10:6)
as indeed it is, but it is not a parable. A parable is marked
by a single story, in strict narrative form, with the entire story
making the point at which the teller aims. In the Synoptic
Gospels the parables are so numerous and so patently original
that we have reason to suppose that they provide, on the
whole, an accurate record of the matter and the manner of
Jesus' teaching.

Apparently the number of parables was very great, far greater,
indeed, than the number of those preserved for us. "With
many such parables he spoke the word to them, as they were

able to hear it; he did not speak to them without a parable, but privately to his own disciples he explained everything" (Mark 4:33, 34). This seems straightforward and clear, but on the question of the fundamental reason for using parables there is a serious problem. Mark announces flatly that the purpose of parables is to confuse the people,[1] and Luke follows him in this, almost word for word (Mark 4:10-12 and Luke 8:9-10). Here is a hard saying, indeed, but it is unambiguous: "And he said to them, 'To you has been given the secret of the kingdom of God, but for those outside everything is in parables; so that they may indeed see but not perceive, and may indeed hear but not understand; lest they should turn again, and be forgiven.' "

Is there any thoughtful person who has ever read this for the first time without a shock? We rub our eyes and look again, convinced that we have made some mistake in reading. Could it be that Christ went to great pains to *keep* people from understanding? If so, this seems to be utterly inconsistent with His character as we find it depicted in other parts of the Gospel. A vast amount of squirming has been done to defend such a policy of arbitrary exclusion, but without manifest success. Certainly this policy is far removed from "Behold, I stand at the door and knock" (Rev. 3:20).

As we try to solve the problem we realize that allusion is here being made to a well-known passage from prophetical writings (Isa. 6:9, 10). That the violence of the paradox bothered Matthew is shown by the double fact that he gets the prophetic word straight by quoting it in full, and also that he changes diametrically the meaning of Christ's statement as reported by Mark and Luke. Whereas these two say "so that they may indeed see but not perceive," Matthew makes Christ

---

[1] H. G. Wood says Mark regards parables as "obscure enigmas." See *Peake's Commentary on the Bible*, (London: T. C. and E. C. Jack, Ltd., 1923), p. 686.

say, "Because seeing they do not see" (Matt. 13:13). We have now no perfect way of knowing which of these is the accurate report, but we do know that, by a slight change, they are rendered opposite to one another.[2]

We are helped somewhat by realizing that the quotation from Isaiah would have been extremely familiar to Christ's listeners, so familiar, indeed, that it would not be necessary for Him to repeat it. It is probable, therefore, that the Matthew account has added the quotation in an effort to solve the problem. As we study the quotation from Isaiah we soon note that it has about it a fundamental ambiguity. We ought to understand this, for sometimes, even today, we employ the paradox of telling people that they are hopelessly stupid, in the hope that the very shock of the announcement will arouse them out of their stupidity. Hopelessness is announced hopefully! We do not know, of course, exactly how Christ said it, since the records are contradictory, but we are probably on the track if we sense the presence of some humor here. It is very likely that Christ's words were meant to be taken in the exact opposite of their literal expression. In that case some would get it and some would not. Humor is an instrument of natural selection.

If this is the solution of a hard problem in exegesis, a problem which is soluble only in the acids of humor, it is by no means unique. We get a strong hint of a similar situation in the account of the two swords (Luke 22:35-38). In this difficult passage, Christ commands a new approach to the world, which is in marked contrast to what has been commanded earlier. Earlier, the Apostles were sent out with practically no equipment, as were the Seventy (Luke 10:1-4), but now the new situation apparently requires a new strategy. The

---

[2] Thus we are bound to conclude that Donald Hankey is wrong when he says that the parable is "almost impossible to distort." *The Lord of All Good Life*, p. 65.

shocking sentence is, "And let him who has no sword sell his mantle and buy one." The naïve response is "Look, Lord, here are two swords." Christ's brief reply to this, the laconic "It is enough," can only mean exasperation. We do not know what He meant, but it is practically certain that the Apostles missed some subtle point which was intended to be obvious. Their mistake must have been that of a humorless literalism. In this regard the confusion about the two swords is similar to the confusion about the purpose of speaking in parables.

That some of the many parables taught by Jesus have become confused is beyond doubt. One of the chief methods of confusion is the insertion into the early, simple parable, of the later teaching and preaching of the Church, so stressed in our day by Professor Bultmann. Bornkamm illustrates this development by reference to the parable of the Great Supper (Matt. 22:1 ff and Luke 14:16 ff). The scholar concludes that Luke, who tells it differently from Matthew, provides the older text, and thus is closer to the original. His chief reason is that, in Matthew, "the telling is strengthened by lurid features."[3] The rich man of the parable becomes a king who sends out his armies to murder the murderous guests and to burn their city. "The extent," says Bornkamm, "to which the Church's faith and theology have formed and added to the tradition of the history of Jesus appears most clearly in the legends and in the story's embellishments, as these increase from one evangelist to another."[4] What is surprising is not that some such embellishment has occurred, so that the parables are not identical in the different versions, but rather that so much remains which is self-authenticating. Among the most reliable features are those which appear as details, but are not reflections of later kerygmatic influence. Of these the humorous

[3] Gunther Bornkamm, *Jesus of Nazareth,* (New York: Harper & Row, 1960), p. 18.
[4] *Ibid.,* p. 19.

touches are the least open to doubt, because they cannot be reflections of serious preaching on the part of overserious men. They must, therefore, be original.

According to Mark's Gospel, which is presumably the oldest and most basic of the accounts, Christ is represented as making His first use of parable in response to the question why His followers acted so differently from the followers of John and of the Pharisees. Specifically, it was noted, as we have stressed in Chapter I of this book, that the Christian fellowship was exceedingly gay. Because the contrast was shocking, the desire for explanation was undoubtedly sincere. The novelty was such that the people simply did not understand. In order to make understanding possible, Christ told the double parable of the patched cloth and of the new wineskins.

New Wineskins

The point of the double parable is transparently clear. To make the point, Christ referred to two of the common elements of everyday life around him, clothing and drink. In each case He insists, by reference to the experience of His hearers, that the change, in order to be effective, must be a radical change. The conviction is similar to one often recognized in our day concerning antibiotics in the treatment of severe illness. A small dose isn't worth anything! Christ illustrates the message of the necessity of the big dose by referring to patched garments and to leather containers of wine. If the fresh, or unshrunk, section of cloth is put on the old and shrunken cloth of the used garment, it will pull away the stitches as it shrinks, and the hole will eventually be bigger than it was before. Even with perfectly good intentions, if we do not have full regard to the tension between the old and the new, our work will end in failure. The inference is that Christ was not patching up the imperfect Pharisaism, but was, instead, instituting something really new.

The example of the wineskins makes the same point in a slightly different form. Wine was contained in the skins of animals, such as goats, and these, for a while, served their purpose well. With the apertures fully closed, they were efficient containers. But the day came, of course, when the skins were old and dried and therefore more vulnerable to pressure from within, especially at the forming cracks. If, in such old skins, new wine were poured, the result would be disastrous, said Jesus. This was because the still fermenting new wine would work and expand and thus bring a pressure on the old, hard, inflexible containers, beyond that which they could bear. Then it was a foregone conclusion that the skins would be burst and both the containers and the contents would be lost.

The clear teaching is that a system like that of the Pharisees is so inflexible that it cannot contain the new fermenting wine of the spirit that is appearing. The system of fasts cannot be reformed; it has to be abandoned and new containers must be found. New vehicles of the spiritual life must be constructed, even though such a step seems bold and shocking. Here, then, as the New English Bible puts it, is the motto of the new movement in the service of the Living God: "Fresh skins for new wine!" (Mark 2:22).

There is a great appropriateness in this double parable at the beginning of Christ's systematic teaching, if it was, as Mark suggests, the beginning. Everyone, including the disciples, is warned at once that what is in store for them is not just a rehash of the old system. They are told, in a method hard to miss, that the new reformation is really a revolution. This will be difficult to keep in mind and their failures will be numerous. "The upshot is," says Bultmann, "that the Old Testament, in so far as it consists of ceremonial and ritual ordinances, is abrogated."[5]

The double parable is thus given, and the point is made. In Mark's account this appears to be the end of the matter, so we turn to an event which illustrates the theme, that of rubbing out the heads of grain on the Sabbath. Matthew follows Mark's account of the double parable faithfully, and then turns abruptly to another story, that of Jairus' daughter. But, fortunately for us, Luke does not end the parable of the wineskins as Mark and Matthew end it. He adds a revealing sentence which is an excellent example of the self-authenticating text, since it certainly is not an insertion reflecting later preaching, and has retained its sly humor, in spite of the obvious tendency to make all things as serious as possible. "And no one after drinking old wine desires new; for he says, 'The old is good'" (Luke 5:39).

We can be grateful to Luke for keeping this delightful touch which, apart from him, we should never have known. It is the real punch line of the story, but, unfortunately, often goes unnoticed. When it *is* noticed there is often a failure to laugh, so that some people actually conclude that Christ is arguing that the old ways are intrinsically better. Once we rid our minds of the false assumption that Christ is always deadly serious, it is not very hard to see what is meant. He says that there must be a new start, that the old methods will not contain the new life that is emerging, *but* we must never delude ourselves that most people will like it this way. Most people will say, "We always did it another way," and they will believe, in their innocence, that what they are using is a clinching argument. Many will arise to say, "The old wineskins were good enough in my childhood, so they are good enough

[5] Rudolf Bultmann, *Primitive Christianity in Its Contemporary Setting*, trans. by R. H. Fuller, (New York: Meridian Books, 1957), p. 74.

now." According to the *Codex Sinaiticus*, the clinching phrase is not "The old is good," but rather, "The old is better." In any case we know that people like the familiar, that they tend to resist change, even when the old ways are clearly failing. How good to know that Christ understood this, and that He said it so slyly, without undue emphasis! Whether the disciples smiled or not we do not know, but we do know that He brings a smile to us now.

A number of people report that they miss the significance of Luke's added line, even failing to be disturbed by the contrast between it and what precedes it, because, in the usual translation, the surprising final sentence begins with the conjunction "and." By changing the beginning Phillips makes the humor more clear. His rendering is, "Of course, nobody who has been drinking old wine will want the new at once. He is sure to say, 'The old is a good sound wine.'" In short, Jesus tells us plainly that He does not even *expect* people to like His new venture; it is altogether too novel and therefore uncomfortable. How thoroughly the humor of the extra sentence can be missed, even by scholarly men, is shown by the following solemn pronouncement in *Peake's Commentary*: "If it was spoken on this occasion it means that John's disciples may rightly continue their own practices." Such is the peril of uncritical solemnity.

Christ's humorous ending should be a great source of comfort and strength to men and women of any generation who are working for some needed, though unpopular, cause. Will people resist us? Yes, says Christ, they will, and this is exactly what we ought to expect. People simply do not like new wine; it is too disturbing to their peace of mind. They like things that are orderly and therefore calculable. The Christian cause, in order to be effective in our day, will need to change in many ways, but we have Christ's word for it that there will be resistance. The teaching of Christ does not lead us to expectations of easy success or of easy lives; it teaches us, rather, to be realistic about human nature.

The parable of the new wineskins is perhaps our best parabolic example of Christ's humor. In thinking of it we see that the humor really sharpens the point already made, that it is not a corny anecdote told for the sake of the joke, but that He is, nevertheless, really joking. The humor comes in quietly, unostentatiously, as an extra dividend which we do not expect. The extreme modesty of the humorous thrust is one reason why it has been so commonly unnoticed. The best of Christ's humor is what we may rightly call "sardonic," and the clearest example of the sardonic thrust is that about the love of old wine.

The Unjust Steward

Though the finest example of humor in the parables of Christ may be that of the wineskins, it is not the most ambitious. The most ambitious example is found in a parable of a totally different character, that of the Unjust Steward. This parable is unique to Luke. It has long been recognized as difficult in interpretation. Dr. Phillips considers the difficulty so great that he provides a treatment of it in the appendix. The problem has been that, though the story is one about a rogue, the ordinary reader feels the necessity of drawing from it some edifying lesson, and this requires more ingenuity than is usually available.

The story is straightforward and clear. It is the account of an employee who was unscrupulous. Word of his personal corruption came ultimately to the ears of his employer, who summarily fired him. After he was dismissed, and before the action was generally known, the scoundrel succeeded in feathering his future nest at his former employer's expense. Recognizing that he was not strong enough to be a common laborer, and being ashamed to be a beggar, he decided to live by his wits, uninhibited by any ethical considerations.

According, the man began to work on accounts receivable and to cause the men who owed bills to be personally indebted to him, even though this meant a loss to his former master. He was, in short, able to earn popularity at no cost to himself, and with no regard for another's consequent loss. If this were the whole story there would be no serious problem, for it is the plain story of a cynical operator, and all are familiar with the type. But this is not the end of the story. Two items follow which have been endlessly perplexing.

The first perplexing item is that "the master commended the dishonest steward for his prudence." There has naturally been some confusion concerning the source of the commendation. Was it the employer or was it Jesus who commended the rogue? In either case, the problem is not easy, though it is much more difficult if we are to suppose that Jesus did the commending. The *reason* for the commending, instead of solving the problem, makes it worse. It may be true, as the text says, that "the sons of this world are wiser in their own generation than the sons of light," but recognition of the simple fact that the unscrupulous are smart is certainly not tantamount to moral approbation of what they do. Whoever did the commending, the reason for the commendation is certainly given in the words of Christ, rather than in the words of the erstwhile employer. The contrast between the children of light and the children of darkness, which appears in this text, has provided the title for one of the most provocative books of the middle of the twentieth century,[6] but what every thoughtful person understands at once is that there is a vast difference between a psychological fact and a moral judg-

---

[6] Reinhold Niebuhr, *The Children of Light and the Children of Darkness*, (New York: Charles Scribner's Sons, 1945).

ment. If we object to a dishonest advertisement and if we are given the reply that it is a financial success, we rightly claim that we have not been answered.

The position which somebody commended has been familiar to literate people since the Renaissance, because of its famous exposition on the part of Niccolò Machiavelli. In short, the cynicism of the leading character in the parable is precisely what we mean by our term "Machiavellian." We must remember, of course, that Machiavelli was merely trying to describe factually how to get ahead, but this is what the steward was trying to do. The steward would have understood perfectly the advice that "injuries should be committed all at once so that, there being less time to feel them, they give less offense, and favors should be dealt out a few at a time, so their effect may be more enduring."[7] But the words of Machiavelli which fit the action of the steward even better are those in which he points out that "spending what belongs to others rather enhances your reputation than detracts from it; it is only spending your own wealth that is dangerous."[8] This is what the steward of the parable understood and practiced.

The second perplexing item is the fact that Christ is represented as advising total unscrupulousness. This is so shocking that it is difficult to see how any literate person has ever been able to read the parable without genuine puzzlement. "And I tell you, make friends for yourselves by means of unrighteous mammon, so that when it fails they may receive you into the eternal habitations" (Luke 16:9). Here is the absolute antithesis of what Christ says in many other parts of the Gospel and, what is worse, it is the exact antithesis of what He is represented as saying in the paragraph which follows

[7] Niccolò Machiavelli, *The Prince*, tr. by Thomas G. Bergin (New York: Appleton-Century-Crofts, 1947), p. 26.
[8] *Ibid.*, p. 47.

immediately. First, He says to feather your own nest and later He says this won't do! In the shocking statement printed above, He even says that the sharp dealing in unrighteous mammon, like that illustrated in the story of the clever rogue, will actually get you into heaven. Then, in the passage immediately following, He says, "If then you have not been faithful in the unrighteous mammon, who will entrust to you the true riches?" (Luke 16:11).

The amount of learned squirming which has been demonstrated in the effort to bring into harmony what is a plain contradiction is phenomenal. Many commentators have tried to say that Christians are admonished to be as wise and clever in the economy of the Kingdom as rogues are in the economy of the world. The usual solution of the paradox is to say that Christ is asking His followers to be smart, to prepare for the future, etc. At the worst, the parable becomes a means of Scriptural defense for the worldliness of the Church and for otherwise damaging compromises with the existing political and economic order. Why, then, shouldn't the clergyman accept bribes in the form of cancellation of parking tickets or even in the form of gifts of fine cars from those engaged in shady business? This is what it means to make friends by means of unrighteous mammon.

There is one, and only one, hypothesis which cuts through all this nonsense of interpretation, with its labored efforts— *the hypothesis that Jesus was joking.* And why not? Since we have already seen abundant evidence that He was joking or teasing on other occasions, there is nothing intrinsically unreasonable about the probability that He is joking in His story of the unscrupulous employee. If we accept this hypothesis, the various perplexities are cleared up! In the first place, it is fair to conclude that it is the employer who is commending the thief in the first response to his recognition of this man's dishonesty. There is no reason to assume that the employer was himself a good man. Perhaps he recognized that he had met his match and, in any case, it is true to say that the steward *was* prudent. That, for which the employer was commending him, was factual. But why, on Christian grounds, should we assume that the prudence is a primary virtue? Indeed, it is not! It may be prudent to be a dictator and to be clever enough to get a reputation as a "Benefactor," but Christ urges a complete transvaluation of such values. It may be prudent to get the best seats, but Christ challenges the entire way of life of which this is one detail. When we are tempted to think that prudence, i.e., self-seeking, is a Christian virtue, we do well to remember that Christ, in His wonderful prayer, thanked the Father that these things, though revealed to babes, were hidden from the wise and prudent (Matt. 11:25, A.V.)

Part of the point of the parable, if it is a humorous one, is that of the necessary transcendence of prudence. It is, in fact, a vivid way of invading the enemy territory in establishing the new ethic. Of course, the unscrupulous are often wiser, or at least may easily appear to be so. Being uninhibited by ethical considerations, they have a marvelous freedom, the freedom *from* moral limitations. Accordingly they can change tactics at any time; they can pay any price required, and as a consequence, may seem very sharp, indeed.

What, then, is Christ saying when He advises His listeners to make friends by means of unrighteous mammon and thereby secure entrance into eternal habitation? He is making a statement so preposterous that the sensitive hearer is supposed to be able to see that the clear intent is the exact opposite of the literal statement. This has been the standard practice in humor ever since Christ's time and, as we have seen, is already illustrated in other parts of the Gospel narrative. But this is, in Christ's teaching, the extreme case. It is so extreme that the people who fail to take it humorously are bound to make themselves seem ridiculous.

Christ is saying, in effect, that if the disciples want to get ahead, they would be wise to cheat in a big way and not fool around with a little. Don't steal *from* the bank, He suggests; steal the bank, and then, instead of being punished, you will be respected. Certainly you will avoid censure if you do it with adequate cleverness and worldly wisdom. Then, to make it more preposterous still, He says it will be a ticket to heaven.

We are fortunate that a very noble passage (Luke 16:13) follows immediately the parable of the Unjust Steward and is normally printed as part of it, even though it is diametrically opposed in teaching. After the humorous banter, which is apparently meant to be transparent, Christ gives His real teaching, to the effect that not even a small degree of unfaithfulness in what belongs to another is to be permitted. We are on high and serious ground when we hear Christ say: "And if you have not been faithful in that which is another's, who will give you that which is your own? No servant can serve two masters; for either he will hate the one and love the other, or he will be devoted to the one and despise the other. You cannot serve God and mammon" (Luke 16:12-13).

This is as uncompromising as can be, whereas the story of the parable is wholly compromising. If the paradox is seriously intended it is unbearable, but if it has a humorous intent, it makes the teaching all the more vivid. We do not know, beyond a shadow of doubt, that the parable is an example of Christ's humor, but we do know that any other hypothesis, of which we can think, leaves the entire matter as an insoluble problem. In view of this, it is surprising to learn how seldom the humorous vein has been detected. Even T. R. Glover, who was so sensitive to humor in other parts of Christ's teaching, apparently did not see the joke in the parable of the Unjust Steward. "How many of the parables," Glover points out, "turn on energy? The real trouble with men, he seems to say, is again and again sheer slackness; they will not put their minds to the thing before them, whether it be thought or action. Thus, for instance, the parable of the talents turns on energetic thinking and decisive action; and these are the things that Jesus admires. . . . Even the bad steward he commends, because he definitely puts his mind on his situation."[9]

Glover's interpretation, in a mood of solemnity untouched by humor, is the standard interpretation, and can be illustrated by reference to the work of many commentators. Thus A. J. Grieve, who at the time of writing was Principal and Professor of Systematic Theology in the Scottish Congregational Theological Hall, Edinburgh, calls the story the parable of "The Shrewd Agent." He mentions the dishonest act by which the steward feathers his own nest at another's expense and then adds, to our great surprise, "That this is at his master's expense has nothing to do with the point of the parable."[10] In short, the commentator thinks he has a clever escape from the moral dilemma by concentrating on the rogue's foresightedness and by minimizing all else. Perhaps this is all that he can do, providing the hypothesis of humor is not accepted or even contemplated, but it makes the whole matter unconvincing. Grieve is representative of many solemn commentators when he says, without a hint of recognition of absurdity, "Unjust gains cannot always be restored to their owners, but they can be given in alms and so win friends or even heaven."[11] This is so far from the Gospel that we are in another world, yet it is to such lengths that men are driven when they operate on the basis of unargued solemnity in Christ's teaching.

One of the most surprising of the solemn accounts of the parable of the Clever Rogue is that of Ernest Fremont Tittle, in his commentary on Luke. His point is the conventional one that the Church can learn from the world, but, accustomed

[9] *The Jesus of History, op. cit.,* p. 130.
[10] Article on Luke in *Peake's commentary on the Bible, op. cit.,* p. 736.
[11] *Ibid.,* p. 736.

as we are to this interpretation, it is hard to take seriously what Dr. Tittle says it is that the Church can learn.

It can learn from entrepreneurs, speculators in real estate, deal-ers in margins! Let the Church look ahead—giving thought to its place and influence in the world of tomorrow, refusing to become so identified with the present social order, with its aims and standards, and material investments, that the disintegration of this order would leave the Church itself discredited and impotent. Let Christians look ahead—knowing that the divine purpose is not confined to the passing world but will have its consummation in a world when death shall be no more.[12]

Much of this sounds very noble, but what Dr. Tittle neglects is that such looking forward is diametrically opposed to the kind of looking forward which the steward of the parable demonstrates. He represents some of the worst features of the social order which Tittle wants to transcend, yet he is com-mended. The conventional interpretation is made with not even a slight indication that there is any felt difficulty. "The Church," we read, "can learn from the world to be resolute and resourceful in the pursuit of its own vocation. If only the Church were as fully committed to the kingdom of God as the world is to the kingdom of money! The world goes 'all out' for the things it believes in. Let the Church, in the pursuit of *its* objectives, be no less determined. The world uses every available medium in selling its goods and putting over its ideas. Let the Church be equally resourceful in promot-ing the things that Christ stands for, using not only the print-ing press but also the radio, the motion picture, even the billboard, perhaps."[13] This is eloquently said, but it is such ob-vious special pleading that we realize that there is nothing too

[12] Ernest Fremont Tittle, *The Gospel according to Luke* (New York: Harper & Brothers, 1951), p. 171.
[13] *Ibid.*, pp. 171-72.

absurd or too evil to be made sermonic material if such an approach is used.

One of the most surprising of contemporary efforts to explain the parable in question is that of Helmut Thielicke, who devotes several thousand words to this task.[14] The device employed by Thielicke is a simple one; he affirms that the real theme of the story is *money*. This enables the author to skip lightly over the major difficulties or even to fail to recognize their existence and to stress the way in which the Christian must learn to use money for good ends. Thielicke imagines the dishonest steward giving away his ill-gotten gains and this, we are blandly told, is what caused him to be received into eternal habitations.

It isn't even *his* money. But this is not the important thing here. After all, he could have burned his master's money or stashed it away for future use. No; he lets it fly. He bestows it upon people who need it. But by so doing he performs a work of mercy and makes friends. In any case, he is above the money and is not a slave to it. He compels the money to perform a service. The money will one day forsake him, but those whom he has helped with it will remain faithful to him and take him in. And this is precisely what Jesus turns into a parable for our own life. This is what he means by the words: "Make friends for yourselves by means of unrighteous mammon, so that when it fails they may receive you into eternal habitations."[15]

It is difficult to read an explanation of this kind without embarrassment. The notion that the steward became generous with his loot is pure fabrication. On the basis of this kind of speculation any message could be tortured out of the text and one would be as good as another. It seems impossible to take

[14] Helmut Thielicke, *The Waiting Father: Sermons on the Parables of Jesus* (New York: Harper & Row, 1959), pp. 93-103.
[15] *Ibid.*, pp. 101-2.

the parable in grave and unsmiling earnestness without falling into pious absurdity.

The record of *The Interpreter's Bible* is a little better than that of most commentaries in that the authors recognize openly that the parable has "nothing edifying about it." That the writers do not accept supinely the conventional unhumorous interpretation is shown by their saying that "since we do not know its original context, we can only guess" the nature of the truth which Christ sought, by this means to make vivid and memorable.[16] Mention is made of the way in which the Emperor Julian made great play with the parable and "said that of course Jesus told it, and of course it proved Jesus mere man and hardly a worthy man." Julian may be bracketed with the philosopher Nietzsche as a critic who assumed, uncritically, that Christ was deadly serious. But, having mentioned difficulties, *The Interpreter's Bible* finally settles for the conventional answer. "Jesus had not commended the steward's dishonesty, but only his prudence. Look at the steward's swift zeal. The worldling thoroughly cares for his senses, while the follower of Christ becomes casual about his soul. The golfer takes lessons and reads books, while the religious man forgets his prayers." All this sounds fine, but by the time it is said the editors must have forgotten their earlier admission that there is nothing edifying about the story. The conventional unhumorous interpretation *is* edifying, but the edification comes at a high price, the price of neglecting the major difficulties. If Christ had wanted to teach the noble lesson that people should be as careful and bold about spiritual matters as about material matters, there are many ways of teaching it without ambiguity. *The Interpreter's Bible* alludes to a score of theories, but does not even mention the one which is most effective in clearing up the confusion.

J. B. Phillips stands out among translators and critics by

[16] Vol. VIII, pp. 280 ff.

the fact that he truly recognizes a problem in the parable of the Unjust Steward, but he never reaches the point at which he entertains the humorous hypothesis. "Most commentators," he recognizes, "suggest that the lesson to be learned is that the follower of Christ should be as shrewd about his spiritual future as the rascally steward was about his own immediate security."[17] This, indeed, has been the almost universal interpretation, but Phillips cannot accept it. "Personally," he writes, "I do not feel satisfied with this view as it introduces a note of careful calculation for the future which is quite at variance with Christ's teaching elsewhere. Moreover, the passage in question goes on to state categorically that dishonesty in earthly things is bound to mean dishonesty in the greater, or spiritual, things, and this seems a very odd conclusion to be drawn from the parable!" It is heartening to know that Phillips sees this, and it is surprising that it is not seen ordinarily.

Phillips struggles hard for an interpretation that will be a valid alternative to the discredited one which we are normally given. In this effort he says that he is attracted to the suggestion of Professor C. C. Torrey, of Yale, to the effect that the original words were uttered in Aramaic and suffered alterations when written in Greek. Professor Torrey, quite as worried as Phillips is, speculated that the most disturbing verses, 8 and 9, may have originally been in the form of questions. "Did the lord praise his faithless manager?" etc. This, though it does not arrive at the possibility of humor, is a step on the way and it intrigues Dr. Phillips. Such a recasting would save appearances, since it would suggest that "even in worldly matters men cannot 'get away with it.'" Phillips' translation, if this drastic solution is to be adopted, would be as follows:

Now did the employer praise this rascally agent because he had been so careful for his own future? For the children of this world

[17] J. B. Phillips, *The New Testament in Modern English* (London: Geoffrey Bles, 1960), p. 255.

are considerably more shrewd in dealing with the people they live
with than the children of light. And do you think I am recom-
mending you to use the false means of money to make friends
for yourselves, so that when it fails you, they could welcome you
to the houses fit for eternity? No, the man who is faithful in the
little things will be faithful in the big things, and the man who
cheats in the little things will cheat in the big things too.[18]

The wonderful integrity of Phillips is such that, though this
interrogative recasting would avoid the inherent scandal, he
will not accept it because it is a distortion of the Greek we
possess. He says that, therefore, "one cannot translate the
statements by questions," and he reluctantly falls back to something perilously similar to the conventional interpretation
which he finds so unsatisfactory. "I have therefore," he writes,
"tried to make the best of it by suggesting that our Lord says,
in effect, that the Christian must 'outsmart' the 'smart' by
turning money, which has so many potentialities for evil, into
a spiritual opportunity." Yet, having arrived sadly at this conclusion, Dr. Phillips still admits that he is not satisfied, and
this is certainly to his credit. He says this "still leaves the following verses about faithfulness rather 'in the air,' "[19] and in
this he is manifestly right. Since he does not mention it, apparently he did not give consideration to the hypothesis that
Christ might be joking.

The amount of self-torture which Christan scholars could
have saved themselves by the mere willingness to contemplate
the possibility of Christ's banter is phenomenal. It is pleas-
ant to think what Glover would have said about the parable
in question if he had applied to it the insight which he applied
to some other reports. "There is a truthfulness and living
energy about all these pictures not least about those touched

[18] *Ibid.*, p. 255.
[19] *Ibid.*, p. 256.

with irony,"[20] said Glover. What a shame that he did not apply this to the one picture in which the hypothesis of humor is most clearly and urgently required.

THE TALENTS

In the two parables just discussed, the humor is reasonably certain and, in any case, the hypothesis does what a good hypothesis is supposed to do: it provides a solution of what is otherwise unsolved. In our third example, however, we are on far less certain ground (Matt. 25:14-30 and Luke 19:11-27). The parable of the Talents, which may also be the parable of "the grasping investor," is one in which humor may or may not be present. The late Edwin McNeill Poteat gave the parable a humorous interpretation, but his lead has not been widely followed by other scholars.

Since it is usually profitable to start with the elaboration of the problem, we may start there in studying the well-known parable of the talents. The parable does not appear in Mark, but it appears in somewhat different versions in Matthew and Luke. In Matthew's version, three servants are given "talents," which were probably worth a thousand dollars each, while, in Luke's version, ten of them were given what we now call "pounds," the word "pound" being used to translate "mina," which was equal to about twenty dollars. According to Matthew, the three servants were given widely different sums to invest, one having five thousand dollars, another two thousand dollars and a third one thousand dollars. According to Luke, however, each was given the same, and a relatively small amount.

Though the two parables thus differ in detail, they involve the same apparent point, *viz.*, that the men make very different uses of their financial opportunities. The men with several

[20] *The Jesus of History, op. cit.,* p. 56.

talents were more thrifty than was the man with a single talent, who returned the investment unimpaired, but also unincreased. The ones who increased the value of the investment were rewarded handsomely, while the ones who produced no increase were severely reprimanded and punished.

The parable, in either form, has, as everyone knows, been the source of countless edifying discourses. The ease of finding a lesson has been increased by the fact that "talents" can be made to stand for our natural endowments, rather than a monetary denomination as in the text. The usual application has been an encouragement to work hard and to make something out of ourselves. In adult Sunday School classes all over the land, this parable has been used as one of the chief supports of the Protestant ethic, and who can say that it has not had some good effects? If there were no more to the parable, we could let it rest, but it is not so simple as we usually make it out to be.

The chief problems are three. In the first place, if the nobleman of the story represents God, as we usually say he does, then the picture of God that is given is very different from the picture which Christ provides in other parts of the Gospel. He is not remotely like Christ and thus the central Christian conviction that God is like Christ seems to be contradicted. In the story, as given by Luke, we learn that the nobleman was hated by the citizens who "sent an embassy after him, saying, 'We do not want this man to reign over us'" (Luke 19:14), and, as we note his spirit, we can only sympathize with them in their desire to be rid of him. Whoever the owner is, he does not represent God in the sense that the father in the parable of the Prodigal Son does. The problem is accentuated by the fact that Luke preserves both of these parables. If God is truly represented by the Father in the story of the Prodigal Son, then God is full of compassion, going out to meet His children when they are willing to return. If, on the other hand, God is

represented by the nobleman in the story of the sharp investment, God is a vindictive usurer. He cannot be both.

The second major problem arises from the preposterous
nature of the rewards. The man who has gained two hundred
dollars in speculation or in exorbitant interest, getting 100 per
cent on his investment, is given, as a reward, "authority over
ten cities." The reward is out of all reasonable proportion to
the benefit rendered. How can we account for something so
obviously disproportionate? But the problem is made even
harder by the fact that the lone pound of the man who did
not speculate is given to the lucky fellow with the original ten.
The people who are watching this extreme action are reported
as remonstrating against such partiality (and they said to him,
"Lord, he has ten pounds!") and we tend to share their con-
sternation. This is a highly revealing touch which Luke has
preserved.

The third problem is involved in the cruel and unusual treatment mentioned at the end of both versions. In Matthew, the
punishment is meted out to the poor fellow whose only crime
is that he did not make extra money for his superior. "And
cast the worthless servant into the outer darkness; there men
will weep and gnash their teeth" (Matt. 25:30). Here is no
compassion, no tenderness, no second choice, no second mile.
We can hardly believe our eyes as we read. But Luke's ending
is even more vindictive and cruel. "But as for these enemies
of mine, who did not want me to reign over them, bring them
here and slay them before me" (Luke 19:27).

What are we to make of these parables? The fact that they
appear, in essential similarity, in both Matthew and Luke
makes it reasonable to conclude that there was an authentic
story which was altered somewhat in the telling and which
may have been affected by its use in subsequent preaching,
prior to the completion of the Gospels. If the two stories as
they now stand are accepted as authentic and serious words

of Jesus, the problems we have mentioned are insoluble. This is why the hypothesis of humor comes as such a relief. If Jesus told a story in a joking mood and the listeners failed to catch the humor, it would be possible to have some such preposterous account as we are actually given. The problem, with this hypothesis, is to see what the nature of the original leg-pulling might have been. In the parable of the Unjust Steward the deliberate use of the preposterous statement is fairly clear, but, with the talents and the pounds, it is not equally clear.

The best guess we can make is that, in the parable in question, Christ is lampooning the popular or conventional conception of God. To this end, God is represented as grotesquely unjust. All men tend to start with this in the light of their experience, which makes them realize that the rich get richer and the poor get poorer. Indeed, Matthew goes out of his way to repeat this observation, already employed in the discussion about the purpose of speaking in parables (Matt. 13:12) and now rendered "For to every one who has more will be given, and he will have abundance; but from him who has not, even what he has will be taken away" (Matt. 25:29).

It is not difficult to see how, in popular thought, the conception of God tends to be that of the hard taskmaster. Life is not easy; injustice is real; men do not have even breaks. In short, the entire problem of evil is involved whenever men try to have an adequate conception of the character of God. The danger is that men will fail to see God in terms of redemptive love, which is as far removed from sentimental permissiveness as it is from harsh vindictiveness. If Christ wanted to overcome the popular view of God as One who is possessive and who plays favorites, the best way to accomplish this might be to make the picture so extreme and the conditions so preposterous that men would begin to laugh at themselves for their former assumptions. They might not see the point if Christ were to talk directly about God, but perhaps they *could* see the point if He were to talk about a grotesquely unjust and mean-tempered man, who used others for his own benefit and who reacted like a madman when he was crossed. This men could see, because they saw it in their own experience and this they would despise, for they hated usury.

If this solution of the multiple problem is correct, the nobleman is not the hero of the story, but rather the villain. He is not a picture of God but, on the contrary, a picture of what God is not. This is not humor in the ordinary sense of the word. It is wry humor and so very subtle that many hearers might not get it. It is no wonder that Christ warned his auditors, "Take heed what you hear" (Mark 4:24), and that, according to Mark, he gave this warning just prior to His statement, which Matthew gives twice, about the apparent injustice of human life. We cannot know for a certainty that the parable of the Talents or the Pounds is based on a humorous teaching, but we do know that a humorless interpretation is intolerable. If it *is* humor, it is closer to the borderline of seriousness than in any other instance which the Gospel preserves.

Thielicke makes the parable of the Pounds into a highly spiritual message, neglecting the harshness of the master. Indeed, he makes the master, representing God the Father, say to the conservative Christian, "You went only halfway; you were lukewarm. You see that's why you did not take me seriously at all."[21] This, of course, is highly edifying, but there is no evidence at all that it is what Christ meant in the parable, and it wholly avoids the problem of divine usury.

There are really only two ways to take a thing seriously. Either you renounce it or you risk everything for it. Either you fling away the pound or you use it and trade with it. There is no third choice. The kind of Christian who is merely conservative and those who

[21] Thielicke, *op. cit.*, p. 145.

want only the Christian "point of view"—these people want this third choice, which doesn't exist. Throw your Christianity on the trash heap, or else let God be the *Lord* of your life; let him be that in dead earnest; let him be someone from whom you receive each day meaning and comfort, a goal for your life, and marching orders, but don't wrap him up in your handkerchief.[22]

This is undoubtedly effective preaching, but its rational connection with the parable of the Pounds is exceedingly thin. Such solemn sermonizing appears to be the only alternative if the possible irony of the parable is not recognized.

[22] *Ibid.*, p. 145.

CHAPTER VI

❧❧

A Humorous Dialogue

> The Canaanitish Woman lives more happily without
> a name, than Herodias with one.
> *Sir Thomas Browne*

IN THE GOSPELS there is little true dialogue. There are numerous examples of humorous paradox and of irony, but not much of the give and take of ordinary conversation. The closest approximation to a true dialogue, which is preserved, is that of Christ's encounter with the Canaanite woman, whose daughter was deranged. Slight as it is, the dialogue is one which haunts us and one which we can never forget, once it has taken hold of our minds. It gives us a view of Christ's character slightly different from what we get in any other human encounter. His reaction to the woman is not the same as his reaction to the disciples of John or to the Pharisees or even to His own immediate followers.

It is extremely heartening to be able to report that, in the experience of the author, there is a more widespread recognition of this encounter as humorous than of any other particular part of the Gospel record. Thoughtful readers are more likely to recognize the humor here than at any other point. This is because they can see that any alternative is intolerable. The account in Mark 7:24-30 is as follows:

116

And from there he arose and went away to the region of Tyre and Sidon. And he entered a house, and would not have any one know it; yet he could not be hid. But immediately a woman, whose little daughter was possessed by an unclean spirit, heard of him, and came and fell down at his feet. Now the woman was a Greek, a Syrophœnician by birth. And she begged him to cast the demon out of her daughter. And he said to her, "Let the children first be fed, for it is not right to take the children's bread and throw it to the dogs." But she answered him, "Yes, Lord; yet even the dogs under the table eat the children's crumbs." And he said to her, "For this saying you may go your way; the demon has left your daughter." And she went home, and found the child lying in bed, and the demon gone.

The theme of the short dialogue which is given in essentially the same form in Matt. 15:21-28, turns on problems of nationality rather than on problems of healing. Luke does not deal with the story at all,[1] but both Mark and Matthew represent Jesus and His closest followers as moving into Phoenician territory immediately after the painful encounter with the Pharisees and scribes who had come from Jerusalem to argue about the law. It was in this particular controversy that Christ had evidently incurred the wrath of His religious enemies by pointing out the dodges which they employed to cover up their failure to keep the whole law. He had also undermined all emphasis on dietary laws (Mark 7:18, 19). Then for some reason, perhaps merely from the desire for rest and change, Christ's little company moved out of the area of greatest controversy into what was considered alien territory.

Mark's reference to Christ's desire to hide makes us conclude that he was tired. "And he entered a house, and would not have any one know it" (Mark 7:24). But, as on other occasions, He could not be hidden. Human need was as great in alien as in Hebrew territory and His reputation of being able

[1] It has been suggested that Luke considered the story unacceptable to his Gentile readers.

to help naturally preceded Him. The one who penetrated His hiding place was a local woman who asked Him to heal her daughter, a person who, in Matthew's version, was "severely possessed by a demon."

All of this is perfectly clear and precisely what previous events would cause us to expect. Then comes something which we do not expect, when Matthew informs us that Christ did not even reply to the woman. In Matthew's account we read, "But he did not answer her a word" (Matt. 15:23). Certainly we do not expect Christ to be rude to the needy stranger. She had, of course, from the strict Hebrew point of view, two strikes against her, being both a woman and a Gentile. In the Hebrew Prayer Book, still in use, the devout worshiper prays, "Blessed art thou, O Lord our God! King of the Universe, who has not made me a woman." But Christ revolutionized thinking about women and the position of women. The change in the attitude to women which stems from the Gospel is one of the finest fruits of His teaching. "His attitude to woman," wrote Glover, "has altered her position in the world. No one can study society in classical antiquity or in non-Christian lands with any intimacy and not realize this."[2]

Scholars have often pointed out the tenderness toward women, and respect for them, which is exhibited in Christ's words and deeds as reported in Luke's Gospel. It is Luke, and Luke alone, who tells us about the women who accompanied Christ as members of the team. "And the twelve were with him, and also some women who had been healed of evil spirits and infirmities: Mary, called Magdalene, from whom seven demons had gone out, and Joanna, the wife of Chuza, Herod's steward, and Susanna, and many others, who provided for them out of their means" (Luke 8:1-3). It is possible that Luke received from these women some of the illuminative stories which he

[2] *The Jesus of History, op. cit.,* p. 125.

alone preserved. But why, when Christ accepted other women, did He not answer the Phoenician? We simply do not and cannot know, for we do not have sufficient evidence. Of one thing, however, we may be sure: it was not because of rudeness or lack of compassion. The love, or "caring," of which the Apostle Paul speaks, and which is clearly a reflection of Christ, "is not arrogant or rude" (I Cor. 13:5). But Christ's initial silence in response to the woman's appeal is not the hardest problem which the story presents. We are told that when the disciples urged Christ to send the woman away, obviously thinking of her as one who was pestering them and their Master, He replied, "I was sent only to the lost sheep of the house of Israel" (Matt. 15:24). Because we are so familiar with the subsequent Christian mission to the Gentiles, associated, in our minds, with the career of Paul, it is hard for us to appreciate or even to understand the Jewishness of the first Christians. Part of the problem lies in the fact that the original proclamation of the Gospel was, in one sense, limited to Israel, yet, in a deeper sense, it already had in it the seeds of the transcendence of all barriers. This latter aspect appeared in Christ's encounter in His home town as represented by the graphic account of Luke (Luke 4:16-30). The latent universalism of Christ's message was precisely that which aroused terrible anger. He affronted his fellow Jews by calling attention to God's tenderness toward foreigners.

"But in truth, I tell you, there were many widows in Israel in the days of Elijah, when the heaven was shut up three years and six months, when there came a great famine over all the land; and Elijah was sent to none of them but only to Zarephath, in the land of Sidon, to a woman who was a widow. And there were many lepers in Israel in the time of the prophet Elisha; and none of them was cleansed, but only Naaman the Syrian." [Luke 4:25-27].

In the message thus given at Nazareth, Christ seemed to go out of His way to include, in His compassionate reference, one who was markedly similar to the chief character in the story we are examining. That is, the person to whom Elijah was said to have been sent, was both a Phoenician and a woman. How, then, could He fail to be compassionate in the contemporary scene? His transcendence of racial barriers rested upon the fact that He faced persons as persons, and therefore could not but be universal in His sympathies. One of the finest examples of the universality of Christ's sympathies is that provided by His encounter with the Roman officer who received a form of approbation higher than that given to any Jew. "I tell you, nowhere, even in Israel, have I found faith like this" (Luke 7:9, N.E.B.).

Another helpful insight is provided by Christ's reference to Jonah. When He was asked for a "sign" He replied that no sign would be given except the sign of Jonah (Luke 11:29, Matt. 16:4). Here Matthew and Luke differ from Mark, who reports Jesus as saying, categorically, that *no* sign will be given (Mark 8:12). It is puzzling, at first, to see any significance in this cryptic reference to Jonah, but we begin to understand when we analyze the purpose of the small Hebrew book in which the character of Jonah is depicted. The central point of the story of Jonah amounts to a lampoon of nationalistic prejudice. Professor Henry J. Cadbury has been particularly helpful in calling the book "A Cartoon of Nationalism."[3] Jonah is presented, in the book named for him, as a man who hates the people of Nineveh so much that he does not even want them to repent. His chauvinism is so grotesque as to be laughable, particularly at the end of the book, which is clearly intended to elicit at least a smile. In view of Christ's evident familiarity with this partly humorous story, it is impossible to believe that He would seriously entertain toward an unfortu-

[3] In his *National Ideals in the Old Testament*.

nate Phoenician the kind of prejudice which Jonah felt for the people of Nineveh.

Once having noted this phase of the message, we must also recognize a contrasting phase, which limits, or seems to limit, Christ's work to the Jewish community. Professor Bultmann emphasizes this aspect more than the one mentioned above.

> But the history of this earliest community itself shows plainly that the teaching of Jesus had not extended beyond the boundaries of the Jewish people; he never thought of a mission to the Gentiles. The mission to the Gentiles came into being only after serious conflicts in the primitive church; and then the assumption was a way of adding to the chosen people, the Jewish Messianic community. The Gentile who wished to belong in the last day to the elect must be circumcised and keep the Jewish Law.
>
> Out of such assumptions arose certain sayings which are put into the mouth of Jesus:
>
> "Go not into any way of the Gentiles, and enter not any city of the Samaritans.
>
> "But go rather to the strayed sheep of the house of Israel." [Matt. 10:5, 6][4]

Bultmann does not neglect the encounters with the Roman officer and the Phoenician woman, but says these stories show that there are exceptions to the general rule.

> We avoid much of the difficulty if we suppose that Christ's first remark to the woman, to the effect that He was sent to the lost sheep of the house of Israel (Matt. 15:24), was not an evidence of harshness, but was, rather, only a restatement of a sense of vocation. But if this is difficult, the succeeding remark is more difficult still. When the woman knelt before Him and appealed, "Lord, help me," His strange answer, as given by both Matthew and Mark, was the implication that

---

[4] Rudolf Bultmann, *Jesus and the Word*, trans. by Louise Pettibone Smith and Erminie Huntress Lantero, (New York: Charles Scribner's Sons, 1934), pp. 43-44.

she was a dog. "It is not fair to take the children's bread and throw it to the dogs."

If there is a harder problem than this in the New Testament interpretation we do not know what it is. Taken at its face value, the sentence is rude and contemptuous. Above all, it is at complete variance with the general picture of Christ which we receive from the rest of the Gospel, particularly in connection with the poor and needy. How can we square this with His acceptance of harlots and taxgatherers and His faith in poor fishermen? A person who does not face this problem, and who is not worried by it, has hardly begun to study the Gospel seriously. As it stands alone, the situation is intolerable, but perhaps the completion of the dialogue can provide us with a clue.

The best part of the confrontation is the woman's sharp and witty reply to the apparent insult, "Even the dogs eat the crumbs that fall from their master's table." It is impossible to miss the humor in the response, even though the Gospel reporters may have missed the humor implicit in *Christ's* words. They had a reason for trying to tone down His humor and to make every remark of His appear to be deadly serious, though in this they could not wholly succeed so long as they were faithful in their account, but they had no reason to make the words of the Gentile woman more serious than they were. The other details in Matthew and Mark differ, but, in the woman's witty reply, they agree. What she is saying is that she may, indeed, be a dog, but even dogs get something, and don't really demand anything fancy.

The clue to Christ's spirit in the entire encounter is His immediate affirmative and friendly response to the woman's wit. He accepted her appeal and consequently her child became the object of His successful attention. The great value of this quick response lies in the way in which it illuminates what went before. If Christ could respond so readily to the banter of another, there is reason to suppose that there was an element of banter in *His* own earlier and apparently insulting statements.

We must remember that words are made very different in connotation by the tone of the voice and by the look in the eye of the speaker. There are things which we can say with a smile, but which cannot be said, without offense, with a straight face. There are numerous words, especially during a period of racial strife, which cannot be said seriously without arousing anger and resentment, but which can be said jokingly, with no harm at all, between those who understand one another's friendly spirit. That Jesus was indulging in this kind of banter about racial and national differences is the only logical alternative to the insufferable hypothesis that He was being intentionally chauvinistic and rude. He could easily have used the epithets with a mock seriousness, yet with transparent irony, and, if so, a keen woman would understand and respond accordingly.

A number of the best scholars have long been driven to the conclusion that the only solution of the problem of the dialogue is a recognition of wit in the encounter. Thus, in Lietzmann's valuable *New Testament Handbook* we read, "Jesus is won, not by the recognition of Jewish primacy, but by the ready wit of the woman." One of the clearest indications, in English, of the necessity of a humorous solution, is that provided by the late Professor H. G. Wood, who produced, for *Peake's Commentary*, both the article on Mark and the article on "The Life and Teaching of Jesus." In his commentary on Mark, Professor Wood writes, "Jesus asserts His conviction that His mission is to the Jews. The assertion is somewhat harsh, only softened by the diminutive 'little dogs,' i.e. household dogs. This must be original. The woman's wit is seen in the way she catches up and builds on the very word which Jesus uses. . . . Mark implies that Jesus yielded out of admiration for the quickness of her answer. . . . This in itself stamps the incident as historical, and throws a valuable light on the person of Jesus."[5]

It is clear that Jesus liked the Gentile woman and responded favorably to her ability to appreciate His real meaning, which was so different from the literal significance of His actual spoken words. He must have laughed at the way in which she engaged in a witty dialogue, of which the part preserved for us is probably only a remnant. *Thus one of the best evidences of Christ's wit is the way in which He responded to the wit of another.*

If the character of Christ, as revealed in the many evidences of His wit and humor assembled in the preceding pages, is authentic, the story of the Syrophoenician woman ceases to present a major problem, and, indeed, comes to be seen as one of the most charming bits of evidence. Anyone who laughs much is bound to appear, at times, lacking in the obvious tenderness which sentimental sweetness of character necessitates. And we know that in some ways Jesus was rough. The reference to "dogs," in the Phoenician dialogue, is not the first which we encounter. Earlier He is reported to have said, "Do not give dogs what is holy" (Matt. 7:6). It was not particularly tender to call Simon "Satan." Epigrams tend to be a little harsh and Christ was evidently replying to the woman by using an epigram, probably one as familiar to her as to Him. The wonderful thing is that both He and she understood and saw the essential inappropriateness of the maxim. There may be some who do not like to interpret the dialogue as a semi-humorous encounter, but, in that case, they are placed in the difficult position of necessarily coming up with a better hypothesis. What is it? If Christ's words in the dialogue are wholly serious, they are a permanent stumbling block to the Gospel. But, if they represent a form of banter, which is consistent

with deep compassion, they give us one of the most delightful
pictures of our Lord which we possess. As in so many other instances of Christ's humor, they shed a light on His character
which otherwise we miss entirely.

When Sir Arthur Quiller-Couch was giving his famous lectures, soon after assuming the Chair of English Literature at
the University of Cambridge, he said, rather surprisingly, "I
suppose that if an ordinary man of my age were asked which
has better helped him to bear the burs of life—religion or a
sense of humour—he would, were he quite honest, be gravelled
for an answer."[6] Possibly that is true. But there is one shining
point in which the professor's ordinary man does not have to
choose and that point is the Gospel of Jesus Christ. It is true
that our common lives are helped by both genuine religion
and genuine humor. In the teaching of Christ the two forms
are conjoined.

[6] Sir Arthur Quiller-Couch, *On the Art of Reading* (New York: Cambridge University Press, 1953), p. 91.

Appendix

Thirty Humorous Passages in the Synoptic Gospels

1. Automatic rewards, Matt. 6:2, 5, 16.
2. No need to borrow trouble, Matt. 6:34.
3. The price of judgment, Matt. 7:12, Luke 6:37.
4. Speck and log in the eye, Matt. 7:34, Luke: 6:41
5. Pearls before swine, Matt. 7:6.
6. Figs from thistles, Matt. 7:16, Luke 6:44.
7. Dead undertakers, Matt. 8:22, Luke 9:60.
8. The insatiable critics, Matt. 11:16-19, Luke 7:31-35.
9. The success of your sons, Matt. 12:27, Luke 11:19.
10. The circumvention of the law, Matt. 15:5, Mark 7:9-13.
11. Blind guides, Matt. 15:14.
12. Bread to the dogs, Matt. 15:26, Mark 7:27.
13. Simon's new name, Matt. 16:18.
14. Get behind me, Satan, Matt. 16:23, Mark 8:33.
15. Big and little debts, Matt. 18:28.
16. Camel through needle's eye, Matt. 19:24, Mark 10:25, Luke 18:25.
17. Begrudging generosity, Matt. 10:25.
18. Follow preaching not practice, Matt. 23:3.
19. Broad phylacteries, Matt. 23:5.
20. Dogs in the manger, Matt. 23:13, Luke 11:52.
21. Straining a gnat and swallowing a camel, Matt. 23:24.
22. The outside of the cup, Matt. 23:25, Luke 11:39.
23. Whitewashed tombs, Matt. 23:27.
24. The gathered vultures, Matt. 24:28, Luke 17:37.
25. Preparation for the thief, Matt. 24:43, Luke 12:39.
26. A lamp under a bed, Mark 4:21.
27. The good old wine, Luke 5:39.
28. Successful pestering, Luke 11:8, Luke 18:5.
29. The unjust steward, Luke 16: 1-9.
30. Rulers as benefactors, Luke 22:25.